Christopher Columbus

and the Age of Exploration for Kids

WITH 21 ACTIVITIES

Ronald A. Reis

CHICAGO
REVIEW
PRESS

Copyright © 2013 by Ronald A. Reis
All rights reserved
First edition
Published by Chicago Review Press, Incorporated
814 North Franklin Street
Chicago, Illinois 60610
ISBN 978-1-61374-674-5

Library of Congress Cataloging-in-Publication Data

Reis, Ronald A.
    Christopher Columbus and the Age of Exploration for kids with 21 activities / Ronald A. Reis. — First edition.
        pages cm
    Includes bibliographical references and index.
    ISBN 978-1-61374-674-5 (trade paper)
    1. Columbus, Christopher—Juvenile literature. 2. Explorers—America—Biography—Juvenile literature.
3. Explorers—Spain—Biography—Juvenile literature. 4. America—Discovery and exploration—Spanish—
Juvenile literature. 5. Education, Elementary—Activity programs. I. Title.

    E111.R37 2013
    970.01´5092—dc23
        [B]

                                                                                                    2013013451

Cover and interior design: Monica Baziuk
Interior illustrations: Jim Spence
Cover images: Map of Columbus trips, iStockPhoto; Santa Maria from Christopher Columbus, iStockPhoto/
Ivonne Wierink; Christopher Columbus, Library of Congress LC-D418-29258; Elements of medieval court life,
ThinkStock/Dynamic Graphics; Christopher Columbus at the royal court of Spain, Library of Congress LC-
USZ62-3939; Slaves cultivating sugar cane in the West Indies, Thinkstock/ Photos.com
Map design: Chris Erichsen

Printed in the United States
5 4 3 2 1

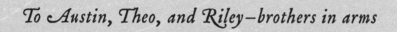

To Austin, Theo, and Riley—brothers in arms

Contents

Note to Readers

THE IDENTIFICATION "INDIAN" TO describe the indigenous people of the Americas has been a source of discussion and dispute in recent decades. The term is historically incorrect since Columbus gave the name to inhabitants of the New World who he thought were the Indians of Asia. Today, the names Native Americans, American Indians, Indians, indigenous Americans, Amerindians, and others, as well as names of specific tribes or peoples, have all found wide use. I use these designations interchangeably throughout the book. Since "Indians" is still the word most often used by the most people, however, that is the term used most frequently here.

The various and sometimes contradictory images depicting Columbus are also worth noting. No painting of the discoverer was made in his lifetime, and no physical description of Columbus written in his lifetime has been found. Portraits of Columbus were painted from descriptions usually written long after his death. However, Friar Bartolomé de Las Casas, who met Columbus in Hispaniola in 1500, gave this description: "As regards his exterior person and bodily disposition, he was more than middling tall; face long and giving an air of authority; aquiline nose, blue eyes, complexion light and tending to bright red; beard and hair red when young but very soon turned gray from labors." Regardless of the variations you will see in portraits of Christopher Columbus, you can rest assured that to those who knew him, he appeared a man of determined bearing and personality.

Acknowledgments

THANK YOU TO AUTHOR Dr. William Wallis for encouragement and support regarding all my writing efforts. Our frequent lunches keep me hungering for more. Thank you to author Dr. LaVergne Rosow for taking such an interest in this book and providing valuable suggestions regarding the activities. Thank you to Dale Beck for being there as my first editor, and as my critic, supporter, and provider of research material. Furthermore, I want to offer a special thank-you to Lisa Reardon, senior editor at Chicago Review Press. From the moment this book idea was conceived, Lisa has been there with the enthusiasm, devotion, and expertise all authors yearn for. Last, but never least, thank you to Karen, my devoted wife, for all you do in aiding my writing efforts.

Introduction

IN 1892, THE WORLD rushed to celebrate the 400th anniversary of Christopher Columbus's arrival in the West Indies—or at least the United States did. In America, the glorification of the discoverer took its most lofty form in the World's Columbian Exposition, held in Chicago. In a nation with 63 million people, the fair attracted 24 million visitors. It cost as much to put on the extravaganza as it would to build the Panama Canal more than a decade later. The Columbian Exposition had but one purpose: to celebrate America's magnificence—a result of Columbus's brave and daring initial voyage, its surprising revelation, and its marvelous impact on world history. Clearly, in 1892, Christopher Columbus held center stage.

Not so 100 years later, in 1992, when the 500th anniversary of the discovery rolled around. No longer, it was said, should Columbus's achievement

The 1892–93 Columbian Exposition in Chicago, Illinois. Library of Congress LC-USZC2-3394

Portrait of Christopher Columbus.
Library of Congress LC-USZ62-9121

be considered an unmixed blessing. Nor should the man himself be viewed with uncritical reverence. Columbus, many historians were now willing to concede, had numerous character flaws that resulted in misadventures and moral failure. He was seen as the first of many Europeans who, in coming to the New World, ravaged the land, plundered its wealth, and eventually introduced African slavery. There was no Columbian Exposition in 1992. In the United States, Columbus was hardly mentioned at all.

Christopher Columbus is possibly the most researched and written-about individual in history. That is not surprising. No matter what one may think of Columbus—hero, heel, or both—the significance of what he did, however interpreted, is monumental. Christopher Columbus changed the world. For that, Columbus, given the title the **Admiral of the Ocean Sea**, deserves to be known and his legacy explored. What follows, hopefully, will be your own act of discovery.

Time Line

First Voyage to the Americas

1492 | King Ferdinand and Queen Isabella of Spain agree to sponsor Columbus; Columbus departs from Palos, Spain, on August 3; arrives in the West Indies on October 12; flagship *Santa Maria* sinks off Hispaniola on December 24; Columbus founds La Navidad on December 26

1493 | Columbus departs Hispaniola for Spain on January 1; arrives at Lisbon, Portugal, on March 3

Second Voyage to the Americas

1493 | Grand fleet of 17 ships departs Cadiz on September 25; Columbus returns to La Navidad on November 28 to find the settlement destroyed and all Spaniards dead

1494 | Columbus arrives at Cuba on April 30; reaches Jamaica on May 5; open warfare breaks out between Spaniards and Indians

1495 | In March, Columbus wins battle on the broad, fertile valley known as the Vega Real

1496 | Columbus departs from Hispaniola for Spain; reaches the coast of Portugal on June 8

Early Years

1451 | Columbus is born in Genoa, Italy. By the age of 14, he takes to the sea

1476 | Columbus swims ashore after his ship is sunk in a battle with a Franco-Portuguese war fleet off Portugal

1480 | Eldest son, Diego, is born

1484 | Columbus conceives of the Enterprise of the Indies; fails to get backing from King João II of Portugal

1488 | Second son, Fernando, is born

1490 | The king and queen of Spain refuse to sponsor the Enterprise of the Indies

1492 | Moors driven from Spain in January

Christopher Columbus sighting the New World.
Library of Congress
LC-USZ62-5339

Third Voyage to the Americas

1498   Columbus departs from Sanlúcar, Spain, with six ships on May 30; reaches Trinidad on July 31; arrives at new city of Santo Domingo on Hispaniola on August 19; Columbus resumes his role as governor

1499   Vasco da Gama, sailing on behalf of Portugal, rounds the southern tip of Africa and reaches India

1500   Columbus arrested in Santo Domingo and sent back to Spain in chains in early October; received, unchained, by King Ferdinand and Queen Isabella on December 17

Fourth Voyage to the Americas

1502   Columbus leaves from Cadiz, Spain, with four ships on May 11; West Indies hurricane on June 30; Columbus arrives at the Mosquito Coast (Nicaragua) on July 30

1503   Sinking ships beached and abandoned at Jamaica on June 25; Diego Méndez and Bartolomeo Fieschi leave for Hispaniola in native canoes on July 17

1504   On June 29, crew rescued from Jamaica after more than a year on the island; Columbus returns to Spain on November 11

1506   Columbus dies at Valladolid, Spain, on May 20

Christopher Columbus, Admiral of the Ocean Sea.
Thinkstock 134100738 (collection: iStockphoto)

Later Explorations

1507   Waldseemüller Map published showing a Western Hemisphere and the name "America."

1513   Juan Ponce de León discovers Florida, thus becoming the first European to set foot on what is now the United States; Vasco Núñez de Balboa reaches the Pacific Ocean by crossing the Isthmus of Panama

1519   Ferdinand Magellan's expedition to voyage around the world begins

1521   Hernando Cortés subdues Aztec Empire

Sundial.
Thinkstock 93611727 (collection: iStockphoto)

ARGONAVTICA.

SAVROMA

Immensa silva GETAE. ARIMASTHAE.

SCYTHAE.

MAEOTAE

ARSOPAE.

MAEOTIS PALVS.

CECRYPHAE.

BASTARNAE. GELO NES.

ALANI. Mirace Hylea

GRAVCENII

TAVRICA. SINTI. CHARANDAEI. CERCETII. BISALTAE. GYMNI

SIGYN NI.

AXENVM Aequor, Iasonio pulsatum remige primum.

CAVCASEVM MARE.

EV RO PAE PA RS

SINDI, CORALLI. Sabyleßius

ASSYRII. PAPHLA GONIA. CHALYBES.

TIBARE NIA.

MACRON

MOSINOECI.

CRO NIVM MARE.

NESTAEI.

THRACIA.

CAPPA DOCIA.

AMAZO NES.

Doeantis, sive Boeantis campus

LIGVRES Alpes montes

ENCHELEAE

PROPON TIS

DOLI ONES

MAVRI DYNI

LATIVM. TYRRHE NIA.

AVSO NIA.

THESSA LIA.

PALLENE

MINOIVM, sur

BEBRYCIA.

Cyrnus Sardo.

TYRRHENVM AEQVOR.

DOLOPES THESSA LIA. Locri. ACHAIA. CVRE TI. CECROPIA.

AEGAEVM Pelagus.

Minoides

ASIAE

THESSA LIA.

DO LOPES

MAGNE SIA. PELASGIA. AEMONIA. LOCRI.

IONIVM MARE.

TRINACRIA.

PELOPIS REGIO.

insulae.

Sporades insulae.

Rhodus

DICTAEVM Mare.

Carpathus

THRACIAE PARS.

PROPON TIS.

LIBYSTICVM MARE.

CRETA.

Ex conatibus Geographicis Abrah. Ortelij Antverp.

CYRENE

Melas sinus

MYSIA. BITHYNIA.

Syrtes, *sive mare vadosum ac arenosum.*

Hesperides. SACER campus

ATLANTICVS Ager.

LIBYAE MERIDIES. PARS.

~ 1 ~

Green Sea of Darkness

For Christopher Columbus there was no doubt. When he set out on August 3, 1492, sailing west into the unknown Atlantic, he had every reason to believe that the ocean he now navigated was the only one on the planet. Furthermore, firm in his belief in a narrow Atlantic, Columbus was convinced he could sail its waters directly from Europe to Asia and do so in just a few weeks.

Yet 30 days outbound from the Canary Islands (where he had stopped to resupply), the crews of the *Niña*, *Pinta*, and *Santa Maria* (Columbus's squadron of three ships) were becoming restless and quarrelsome. As experienced and competent seamen, many felt their captain had gone far enough without sighting land. It was, they cried, "time to turn back."

But Columbus was determined to stay the course. According to the captain's calculations, the wealth of the Orient lay just a few more days ahead. The Enterprise of the Indies, as his endeavor was named, had to keep going.

Sea monster. Thinkstock 92241969 (collection: iStockphoto)

The journey so far had not been particularly harrowing. Yet the uncharted Atlantic was a threatening place, especially this far out from known land. The ocean all around the sailors could often seem "a Green Sea of Darkness," the term used by medieval Arabs to describe its terrors.

And dread there certainly was.

Throughout the Middle Ages and well into the Age of Exploration that Columbus embraced, tales abound of an Atlantic filled with imaginary beasts and fabulous monsters. "There were men without heads, with their faces on their chests," one text assured. "There were men with the heads of dogs, one-legged men with one gigantic foot apiece; there were giants and dwarfs, harpies [mythological creatures, half women, and half bird] and dragons." These monsters were described in wildly imaginative travelers' tales and shown on maps as living on islands outside the known world.

To calm his crews' nerves and to stave off a possible mutiny, Columbus made a deal with them on October 10. If land was not sighted within three more days, he would end the mission and turn around for Spain. To keep the crews vigilant and ever on the lookout, Columbus offered the first man to sight land a silk **doublet** (jacket), to be given later. This would be in addition to what the queen and king of Spain, Isabella and Ferdinand, had already promised the first seaman to spot *terra firma* (solid earth).

It was at this time, with everyone eager to locate land, that a false alarm was heard—from the captain, no less. An hour before moonrise, at 10:00 PM on the evening of October 11, Columbus, standing at the **stern** (rear) of his **flagship**, the *Santa María*, thought he saw a light. "So uncertain a thing that he did not wish to declare that it was land, but called a seaman to have a look, and he thought he saw it, too." The light, Columbus later insisted, "was like a little wax candle rising and falling."

Whatever Columbus spied, it was not land. His ship was, at the time, 35 miles from any coast. Still, exhausted but exuberant, the captain laid a course straight for what he thought he had seen.

At about 2:00 AM on October 12, Rodrigo de Triana, a seaman on the *Pinta*, saw something resembling a white sand cliff under the light of the nearly full moon. Then there was another. A dark line connected the two. Triana cried out, "Terra! Terra!" (Land! Land!). Columbus and his ships were six miles from the New World.

The sovereigns of Spain had promised a life pension of 10,000 *maravedis*, a generous sum, to the first one to glimpse land. But Triana was denied the reward. Columbus, insisting that he had seen land four hours earlier, received the money. Triana received nothing.

In an undertaking to find a fast, direct water route to Asia from Europe, the three "Gs" (God, gold, and glory) were what propelled Christopher Columbus forward. In claiming the 10,000 *maravedis*, cheating Triana out of his just due, Columbus momentarily set aside God and even gold (the money), and thought only of glory. He could not bear to think that anyone but him would be credited with identifying land first.

Born to the Sea

FOR THE past 100-plus years, much questioning regarding Christopher Columbus has taken place. At times it can seem everything the admiral ever did,

*Christopher Columbus and his crew in the **Santa Maria** ship looking for land.*
Thinkstock 98954826 (collection: Dorling Kindersley RF)

along with why he did it, is being looked at in a new way. Such suspicion even extends to Columbus's place and date of birth.

Some historians stretch the possible dates of Columbus's birth from as early as 1436 to as late as 1455. Most scholars, however, insist he was born between August 25 and October 31, 1451.

Where Christopher Columbus was born is of greater certainty. It was almost assuredly in the bustling maritime city of Genoa, one of many Italian coastal city-states. Genoa, situated as it is on the western side of the Italian peninsula, was an ideal place for a young lad with seafaring desires to grow up. This was especially true for one who would look west, not east, for exploration and adventure.

Christopher was born the first of five children. Of his three brothers, two remained close to him throughout his life and contributed significantly to his success as an explorer. Bartolomeo, born in 1453, shared in almost all of Christopher's sea adventures. Giacomo (Diego), was born 17 years after Christopher, but he also took to the seas with his much older brother. Later, he sought to protect Columbus's interests in the Spanish court.

Columbus's father, Domenico Colombo, was a wool weaver and tavern keeper. Columbus's mother, Susanna Fontanarossa, was the daughter of a weaver. Christopher, who was actually born Cristoforo Colombo (his Italian name), grew up working in the wool trade. Except, that is, when he was out seafaring, which was often. As early as the age of 10, Christopher plowed the Genoese harbor, solo, with small borrowed sailboats.

Though Domenico never achieved any degree of wealth, he was an optimistic and kind fellow who provided a modest living for his family. It was said of him that, "He was the type of father who would shut up shop when **trade** was poor and take the boys fishing; and

Medieval seamstresses making clothes.

Thinkstock 104571580 (collection: Dorling Kindersley RF)

CRAFT A SEA NEREID (GODDESS OF THE SEA)

ACCORDING TO his son Ferdinand, Columbus was intrigued and delighted by fables and stories he heard about sea creatures. One such creature was the Greek Nereid ("wet one"). Nereids were mythical sea nymphs, daughters of the nymph Doris. There were 50 of them, all of whom frolicked on the surface of the water and lived in the underwater palace of their father, Nereus, at the bottom of the Aegean Sea. Nereids had golden hair and a golden throne in their father's palace. They often rode on dolphins. Nereids were considered the patrons of sailors and fishermen, and they came to the aid of men in distress.

In ancient art, Nereids were depicted as beautiful young maidens, sometimes swimming with small dolphins or riding on their backs. They could also be seen in the presence of other marine creatures, such as sea horses.

In this activity, you design and create your favorite Sea Nereid. For further information and ideas regarding Sea Nereids, see these websites:

www.theoi.com/Pontios/Nereides.html
www.pantheon.org/articles/n/nereids.html
http://ancienthistory.about.com/od
/godsandgoddesses/a/Nymphs.htm

Materials

✢ Pencil
✢ White poster board
✢ Colored pencils, crayons, or markers
✢ Scissors
✢ Glue
✢ Construction paper; various colors
✢ Embellishments such as beads, feathers, foam shapes, yarn, tiny trinkets, dots from a hole puncher, filings from a pencil sharpener, pencil stubs and eraser bits, bottle lids, colorful leaves, broken toy parts, spools from paper towels and toilet tissues, old combs, hair from the barber shop.

1. Before you begin, spend some time thinking about what your Sea Nereid will look like.

2. Sketch an outline of the Sea Nereid on the poster board. Use pencil so you can alter your design until you're happy with it.

3. Use colored pencils, crayons, markers, or cut-out shapes from construction paper to add color.

4. Use embellishments to decorate her—perhaps a gown; crown, tiara, or headdress; scepter; jewelry; and so on. Have fun putting together your design for a Sea Nereid and be sure to give her a name.

Your teacher may want you to stand up in class and present your Sea Nereid. Describe what your Sea Nereid means to you.

the sort of wine seller who was his own best customer."

A physical description of Christopher as a boy and descriptions of his personality while growing up are hard to come by. As a youth, given his physical energy, he must have been attractive and energetic. As a man, he was considered of medium height, neither fat nor thin.

A trace of young Christopher's personality can be gleaned from the fact that as a man, he failed to do what almost every seaman of his time, and since, has done—curse and swear. His son Fernando later said that he never heard his father utter any other oath than, "By San Fernando!" When angry, Columbus would simply cry out, "May God take you!"

Little is known about Columbus's schooling. He may never have gone to school at all. When Columbus left home (sometime around his 20th birthday) he might have been illiterate—unable to read or write. While it was said of Columbus that "growing up he was of great intellect but little education," the young Genoese man educated himself. He gained knowledge of math and mapmaking, to say nothing of the Latin, Spanish, Portuguese, and Genoese languages. And Columbus eventually learned to read and write.

Fourteen is the age usually given for Columbus having first gone to sea. If that is true, then 1465 was the year of his plunge into seafaring. For a half-dozen years after that, Columbus served on various ships in various roles, working as a messenger and a common sailor. At the age of 21 he may even have become, if only briefly, a pirate of sorts.

According to legend, in 1472, Columbus was in the service of Duke René of Anjou. The duke had appointed Columbus to lead a crew as their captain to capture a **galleass** (warship) in the harbor of Tunis, across the Mediterranean in North Africa. Columbus's crew, however, lost their nerve. They wanted to return to Marseille, France, to gather reinforcements.

It was at this moment that Columbus hit upon a trick to deceive his men. Columbus is said to have tampered with the ship's compass so that in the dark the ship sailed south instead of north. "I made sail at night and the following day at daybreak we were already within Cape Carthage," he later wrote. "The crew had all taken for granted that we were heading for Marseilles."

Most scholars are of the opinion that Christopher Columbus, as good a seaman as he had become, would never have been given command at the age of 21 of such an expedition.

More credence can be given to a voyage Columbus took two years later, in 1474. Here he was hired as a sailor on a ship bound for the Greek island of Khíos, in the Aegean Sea.

✠ Phoenician Sailors and The Mediterranean Sea

Mediterranean means "the center of the world." There is little doubt that those who lived along its shores, from ancient times to the Age of Exploration in the 15th century, saw the sea as such. To them, the Mediterranean's mild climate was a natural aid to the development of higher civilization. And their civilizations, be they Egyptian, Mesopotamian, Palestinian, Phoenician, Greek, or Roman, were seen as central to all that existed.

The Phoenicians, based in what is now Syria and Lebanon, were the great sea-traders of the ancient world. They were the first to take to the Mediterranean in large ships. Such vessels were designed and built to carry trade goods. Occupying only a small strip of land in what is now Lebanon, the Phoenicians had little choice but to branch out, explore, and conquer the Mediterranean.

Since the Phoenicians inhabited the eastern portion of the sea, exploring Mediterranean trade routes meant heading west. In doing so, the Phoenicians took three routes:

The northern passage took them through Turkey, Greece, Corfu, the heel of Italy, the Italian coastline to Elba, then across to Corsica and Sardinia. The Phoenicians traveled in ships powered by sails and crews of oarsmen. They hugged the coast, and sailors often went ashore at night to drink and sleep.

Southern convoys followed the North African coastline. The ships always stayed within sight of land. It is said that many a port on today's maps represented one day's sailing from the next for Phoenician ships.

The third course taken, which came later, meant going straight out to sea. The ships sailed beyond the sight of land. These voyages required more sophisticated sailing equipment, navigational aids, and experienced seamen.

Phoenician ships clearly sailed beyond the **Pillars of Hercules**, or what is known as the Strait of Gibraltar. Phoenician seafarers visited the Canary Islands. However, even though they surely sailed farther west and far out into the gray Atlantic, of this there is no direct evidence, only speculation.

The Mediterranean Sea. Thinkstock (photographer: Hemera Technologies) 89763922. (collection: AbleStock.com)

A Renaissance sculpture.

Thinkstock 145999987 (collection: iStockphoto)

Columbus, after this first long voyage, spent a year on Khíos. Christopher Columbus's trip to this island brought him the closest he ever got to Asia.

Rebirth

CHRISTOPHER COLUMBUS, a man of the last half of the 15th century, had one foot in medieval Europe (the Middle or Dark Ages) and one foot in a new age dawning—the Renaissance. With the fall of ancient Roman civilization in the fifth century, a dark age befell Europe. The glories of Greece and Rome remained buried for centuries. The arts, science, study of nature, and freedom to investigate were all suppressed. With the coming of the Renaissance (French word for rebirth), the beginnings of modern art and science took hold. Men like Michelangelo, Leonardo Da Vinci, and Johannes Gutenberg were leaders in the rebirth and discovery of ancient ways. They were also part of creating new ways of doing things. So, too, was Christopher Columbus.

Renaissance or not, however, the vast majority of European citizens continued to live a brutal, unstable, and short existence. Outbreaks of plague, torture of citizens, and religious inquisitions against the Jews and Muslims kept everyone on edge. Pits of sewage and mass graves provided a breeding ground for disease. Most of the population rarely took baths. Wars, crime, and riots added to the general misery. Life could be short and brutish. A person in his or her 40s was considered old and lucky to still be alive.

Fortunately, though, Genoa, where Columbus was born, was teeming with all that the **Renaissance** represented. For years it had been carrying on victorious wars with other Italian seaports, all the better to expand its commerce. The city had grown so rich, with so many marble churches and palaces, its people referred to it as "Genova la Superba" (Superb Genoa).

Trade, the exchange of goods and services, was, at the time of Columbus's birth, taking place all across the Mediterranean Sea. Much of that trade made its way east to Constantinople (modern Istanbul, Turkey). European goods then went by land as far as Asia. Goods of Asia made it back to Europe in the same way. This splendid exchange had been going on for centuries.

In 1453, two years after Columbus was born, the European/Asian trade, via Constantinople, suddenly ceased. The Ottoman Turks overran Constantinople, smothering the Orthodox Christian Byzantine Empire headquartered there. European merchants could still buy Asian goods. But to do so, they had to deal with Muslims in places such as Alexandria,

Egypt. Christian Europe did not like to do this. It longed to go it alone, to find a way to bypass the Muslims and trade directly with Asia. The only way that could happen was to find an all-sea route to the Orient. The first European country to do that would gain a monopoly on such trade. It would become rich—very rich.

Breaking the Barrier of Fear

PORTUGAL WAS the European country in the best position to begin the search for a water route to Asia—via India, China, or Japan. The country had at least two advantages. Unlike its rival Spain, Portugal was a united kingdom for the whole of the 15th century. It was hardly touched by civil disturbances. In addition, its geography was ideal. Portugal's entire coastline was on the Atlantic Ocean. All its harbors, deep and wide, opened oceanward. The Portuguese people faced outward, away from classical Europe and toward an unfathomed ocean, not to the Mediterranean—the "Sea-in-the-Midst-of-the-Land."

To find a waterway to Asia, the Portuguese were determined to head south, down the west coast of Africa. No one knew how many miles the journey would take them. No one knew the shape of the African continent. And no one knew where it could be rounded.

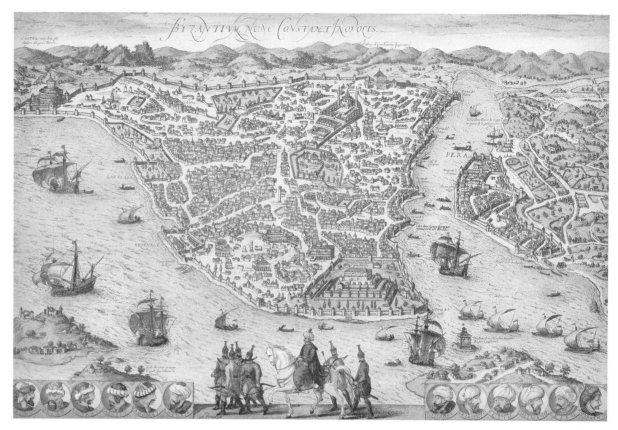

Old map of the Ottoman Turk Empire.
Thinkstock (photographer: Hemera Technologies)
87619747 (collection: AbleStock.com)

What the Portuguese did know is that finding that route to Asia would take time, money, and tremendous effort. It would require a national commitment. For that to happen, the Portuguese needed a leader with vision and uncompromising dedication. In the early decades of the 15th century, Portugal found such a visionary in Prince Henry the Navigator.

Born in 1394, Prince Henry was not a very engaging person. He lived like a monk. He

A caravel, Christopher Columbus's favorite type of ship.

never married. And he never displayed any **dynastic** ambitions. Furthermore, though key to the Portuguese years of discovery and adventuring, Prince Henry never took to long sea voyaging himself. He forever remained the behind-the-scenes guy, a person who provided money and support for the enterprise but did not directly participate himself.

In 1416, Prince Henry set up shop, so to speak, at Cape St. Vincent, on the southwestern tip of Portugal. In a sense, what the prince created there was a primitive research and development laboratory.

During the next decade, Prince Henry gathered around him experts in many fields. New instruments for navigation were invented. The **caravel** ship was created. Using a new design, such a ship could sail into the wind. The caravel could not only go out exploring, it could also come back. The vessel was designed specifically for discovery.

In wave after wave, Portuguese caravels plowed south, hugging the African coast. They did so, that is, until they came upon Cape Bojador, a tiny bulge less than a thousand miles from the home country. Call it superstition. Call it precaution. Call it just plain fear. No one wanted to go beyond the cape. Between 1424 and 1434, Prince Henry sent out no fewer than 15 expeditions, all with instructions to break through the imaginary barrier and con-

tinue on. Each returned with an excuse as to why they could not, would not, go further.

Finally, at the end of 1434, a sea captain named Gil Eannes took a chance. He passed beyond Cape Bojador, thus breaking the barrier of fear. Eannes and his crew were no worse for the effort.

The Portuguese continued on their way, proceeding year by year ever farther south, then east for awhile, then south again, eventually crossing the equator.

With the death of Prince Henry in 1460, there was a momentary pause in Portugal's push southward. When exploration resumed, the goal was immediate and urgent—round the African continent and head for Asia.

In August 1487, Bartholomeu Dias, with two **caravels** and a supply ship, sailed out from Lisbon Harbor. He was determined to find a way around Africa.

Dias crossed the equator and proceeded down the west coast of Africa. As he did, a storm came up that battered his squadron for 13 days. The ships were driven far from shore, into the open ocean.

After the storm, Dias sailed east, still out of sight of land. Then, on February 3, 1488, the explorer anchored in Mossel Bay. He was about 230 miles east of what is now Cape Town, South Africa. Dias had rounded the Horn of Africa.

The captain wanted to keep going and work his way across the Indian Ocean to India. His crew, however, would have none of it. Weary and terrified, they insisted that Dias turn around. They desperately wanted to go home. Hadn't they done enough already? they reasoned.

Bartholomeu Dias did not make it to India; that would have to wait for Vasco da Gama, 10 years later. Nonetheless, Dias made it back to Portugal, where he was summoned by King João II to report his findings. There to witness the event was Christopher Columbus. He is said to have sat glum faced. That Portugal now had a clear sailing route to Asia had a great effect on Columbus's plans.

The Atlantic Beckons

HAVING BEEN born in Genoa, Columbus was bound to look west, not east, for his seafaring exploits. Though located on the Mediterranean shoreline, Genoa faces to the west, toward the **Pillars of Hercules** (the Strait of Gibraltar) and the cold, gray Atlantic beyond. In 1476, Columbus had his first opportunity to leave the relatively calm Mediterranean Sea and enter a true ocean.

In May of that year, a commercial expedition consisting of five ships left the port at Genoa. They were bound for Lisbon, England,

---

✠ The Silent Trade

As Portuguese explorers sailed ever farther down the west coast of Africa, rounding its bulge and proceeding eastward, they encountered bountiful trading opportunities. Of course, the Africans had been trafficking among themselves for centuries. The kingdom of Ghana was particularly well situated to take advantage of the rich exchange of goods.

To facilitate trade among people who did not speak each other's language, a curious method, known as "the silent trade," developed. After a difficult three-week journey across the Atlas Mountains, Muslim caravans from the north would arrive in Ghana.

There, usually on a beach or other open area, the Muslims laid out separate piles of salt, beads, and manufactured goods. Then they retreated out of sight. The local tribesmen, who had acquired gold from a variety of sources, then appeared to place the precious metal beside each pile of Muslim goods. They, too, now backed off, out of sight.

The Muslim traders either took the gold offered or reduced their piles of goods to what they thought was a fair exchange. Once again the Muslims withdrew, and the process repeated itself until agreement was reached. Without speaking a word, trade took place.

When the Portuguese arrived, it didn't take them long to see the advantages of the silent trading system. Among those who did not understand each other's spoken words, there really was no other way to make an exchange. If one side or the other just grabbed goods and took off, it would result in only a one time advantage. All trade would cease thereafter.

---

and Flanders. Columbus was on one of the five ships, probably the *Bechalla*. He traveled as a common seaman.

Upon rounding the Cape St. Vincent, all five ships were attacked by a Franco-Portuguese war fleet of 13 or more vessels. Both sides lost ships. Though outnumbered, the Genoese proved no easy prey. The battle lasted all day.

DEMONSTRATE THAT THE EARTH IS HOTTER AT THE EQUATOR

CHRISTOPHER COLUMBUS and other explorers of his time knew that the round earth was hottest at the equator. They knew that as one traveled away from the equator, going north or south, it got cooler. They may not have known why, however.

The main (but not only) reason that the equator is hotter than the rest of the planet is not, as one might first assume, because the equator is physically closer to the sun than the North or the South Pole, for example. It is because as the sun strikes the earth at the equator, the earth curves less in the equatorial region. While the sun is overhead at the equator, its rays slant as one moves either north or south. The sun's rays are more concentrated at the equator.

As shown below, where the flashlight represents the sun, area X receives the same amount of sunshine as area Y, which is at a higher latitude. But since the light shining on area Y is more spread out, it is less concentrated than at X. The more concentrated the sun's rays, the hotter it will be. In other words, for the same area (say one square mile), the amount of sunshine received is greater at X than at Y.

The same principle is demonstrated below. As one moves north or south from the equator, the sun's rays are more spread out and, as a result, there is less heat within a given area.

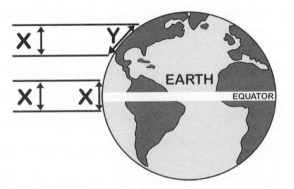

You can demonstrate the effect just described with a globe and flashlight.

Materials
✦ Globe
✦ Flashlight

1. Place the globe in a darkened room.

2. Turn on your flashlight and aim the beam at the earth's equator. Hold the flashlight approximately 3 to 4 inches from the globe. Notice the circle of light hitting the earth.

3. Now raise the flashlight slowly upward, while keeping it in a horizontal position. See how the circle of light changes to an oval of light: the farther you move up toward the North Pole, the more the oval stretches out, and the less concentrated the light is. The amount of light coming from the flashlight (sun) is still the same, but as you move up (north), it gets more spread out.

4. Try moving the flashlight down from the equator, to the South Pole. Are the results the same?

Other factors, such as the amount of atmosphere and the reflectivity of the earth's surface, also affect how hot it will be at any location on our planet. Mainly, though, where you are on the earth will determine how hot it is.

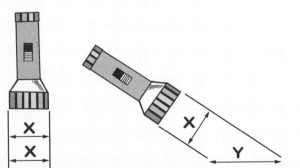

In the end, three Genoese ships and four of the enemy's ships went down. Hundreds of men drowned.

Since one of the ships to sink was the *Bechalla*, Columbus would have drowned, too, had it not been for a lucky break. The seaman, wounded, dove into the ocean, grasped an oar that had floated free, and by pushing it ahead of himself and resting on it, he was able to reach shore, at Lagos, Portugal, more than six miles distant.

The people of Lagos treated Columbus well. After recuperating, he made it to Lisbon. There he settled in with the large Genoese colony of merchants and shipbuilders. Being stuck in Portugal proved to be advantageous for the man from Genoa.

In the following year, the young seaman shipped out of Lisbon, on a voyage bound for Iceland. Columbus noted that Iceland lay "much beyond the limit of the West." The budding explorer may already have been thinking about the East.

By the spring of 1477, Columbus was back in Lisbon. Portugal's bustling port city was the world center of oceanic voyaging and discovery, and Columbus was now living among people who could teach him everything he was eager to learn. Having learned to read and write, he acquired abilities in Portuguese and Castilian, the languages of far-ranging seamen. He learned Latin in order to read the geographi-cal works of the past. He studied mathematics and astronomy for celestial navigation. And, of course, there was shipbuilding and rigging to observe.

In 1478, Columbus again took to the sea. He visited the three major Atlantic **archipelagos** (groups of islands). The Azores were 800 miles west of Portugal. The Madeira group was 450 miles from Morocco. And the Canaries were just 100 to 200 miles west of the African coast. All played a vital role in Columbus's future.

Love and Marriage

THE FOLLOWING year, 1479, Columbus met and married Felipa Moniz Perestrello. If Columbus's son Fernando is to be believed, the two had one of the shortest courtships in history. "A lady named doña Felipa Moniz, of noble birth and superior of the Convent of the Saints, where the Admiral used to attend the mass, had such conversation and friendship with him that she became his wife."

The convent Fernando speaks of was actually a fashionable boarding school attended by young women of nobility. Felipa, 25 at the time, was considered old to be unmarried. And though she was of noble birth, with family connections to the Portuguese court going back

Tie Nautical Knots

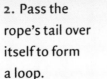

BOAT (SAILING) knots have been used for centuries for handling heavy loads when berthing, mooring, and towing another vessel, as well as in preparing for a storm or managing sails. Columbus and his crews needed to know how to tie a dozen or more knots of various kinds.

With nautical knots, the emphasis is on being able to use the rope over and over again, and to untie each knot without difficulty. In many knots, there is a standing end and a tail end. The former takes the strain; the latter is the loose end in your hand.

In this activity you are shown how to tie two relatively simple nautical knots: the square knot and the sheet bend knot. For instructions on how to tie many more nautical knots, see Animated Knots by Grog, at www.animatedknots.com.

Materials

✣ 2 pieces of rope, preferably of different colors, each at least 1 foot long

TYING A SQUARE KNOT

1. Lay out a rope, as shown.

2. Pass the rope's tail over itself to form a loop.

3. Continue under and around the standing end of the rope.

4. Complete the knot by passing the tail of the rope through the loop.

TYING A SHEET BEND KNOT

1. Lay out two ropes, of different colors if possible, say one light and one dark. Place them in an "S" shape.

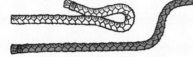

2. Form a loop in the light (unshaded) rope. Hold it in one hand.

3. Pass the dark (shaded) rope through the loop in the light (unshaded) rope.

4. Pull the dark (shaded) rope through a few inches.

5. Bend the dark (shaded) rope behind the light (unshaded) tail and standing ends in that order.

6. Tuck the dark (shaded) rope under itself to finish the knot.

generations, Felipa was not wealthy, and she had no dowry to offer. Fortunately, Columbus did not demand one.

Felipa's father, Bartolomeo Perestrello, had been governor of Porto Santo in the Madeira Islands. Soon after the marriage, the couple settled in Porto Santo. Columbus and Felipa then moved to the largest island in the Madeira group to make a home. It was here their son Diego was born, in late 1480. It was also where Felipa died soon after. The actual cause and date of Felipa's death is in dispute. Some have suggested she died of tuberculosis. With her death, Felipa disappears from history. Columbus, in all his writings, never mentions her again.

In late 1481 or early 1482, Columbus sailed south from Lisbon, along the western coast of Africa. He stopped at the Portuguese fortress of Elmina, in what is now Ghana. It was a useful and educational trip for Columbus.

Christopher Columbus had, by now, years of experience sailing the Atlantic Ocean. He had gone as far north as Iceland. He had traveled south to Ghana. He had not, however, pro-ceeded directly west, out into the "Green Sea of Darkness." Who knows, Columbus must have thought, what traveling in such a direction might reveal?

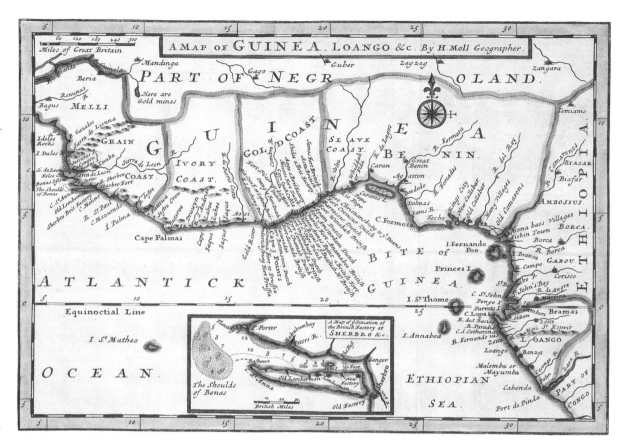

Antique map of Guinea and adjacent African nations.
Thinkstock (photographer: Hemera Technologies)
87725586 (collection: AbleStock.com)

~ 2 ~

The Enterprise of the Indies

THE WORLD IS NOT flat. Today, everyone knows that. In Columbus's day, more than 500 years ago, most educated people knew it, too. The idea that a ship could sail away only to fall over the earth's edge and be carried down an endlessly wide waterfall to who knew where was a bit absurd. Evidence of a spherical world was all about for anyone to see—all one had to do was look.

The Greeks may have been the first to make serious observations, more than 2,000 years ago. The philosopher Aristotle (384–322 BC) argued that the earth was a sphere because during a **lunar eclipse**, the shadow of our planet cast a round edge on the moon. The only solid that always projects a round edge is a sphere.

Furthermore, the Greeks noticed that star constellations shifted relative to the horizon as one moved north and south about the globe. Indeed, the North Star completely disappeared when a person, going south, crossed the equator. This could only happen if an individual was on a sphere.

While the ancients knew little about gravity, its existence explains why the earth, as well as the planets and the sun, are spherical. With a spherical body, every point on its surface has the same distance from the center. Thus it has the same gravitational pull. Even with slight height variation for mountains and valleys, this is true for our planet as it is for others.

In the third century BC, the Alexandrian philosopher and mathematician Eratosthenes went a step further regarding a spherical Earth—he sought to determine its actual circumference. When his measurements were in, Eratosthenes had succeeded in calculating the earth's dimensions with amazing accuracy.

Using the process of deduction, Eratosthenes first chose a city in Egypt, Syene (Aswan today), where on the solstice (when the sun is directly overhead on June 21) the solar rays cast no shadow at noon. Then the philosopher selected another city, 500 miles to the north, Alexandria. If the sun was directly overhead at Syene, Eratosthenes reasoned, it could not also be overhead at Alexandria. With the city to the north, the sun would have to cast a shadow at an angle.

Eratosthenes understood that by determining the angle at Alexandria and then multiplying it by the distance between the two cities, 500 miles, he could come up with the earth's circumference.

The angle turned out to be a little more than seven degrees. That made it one-fiftieth of a full 360-degree circle. Thus the circumference of the earth had to be 50 times 500. Doing the simple math, Eratosthenes came up with an Earth 25,000 miles in circumference. Today, we know our planet to be 24,901 miles around at the equator. Eratosthenes's calculation was unbelievably on target—he was off by less than 1 percent.

Even before the Greeks it was possible for anyone, particularly a person living near the sea, to see for him or herself that the world was a sphere. If one stands on the seashore and watches a ship sail off to the horizon, the ship will be seen to gradually disappear from view. It's not just distance that makes the ship eventually fade from sight. A keen observer will notice that the **hull** of the ship vanishes first. The sails and mast will disappear a bit later. The ship is dropping behind a hill so to speak, the hill being the curvature of the earth.

The situation is reversed for a sailor coming home. A sailor atop the mast of the ship will see land before a shipmate on the deck does. Indeed, that is why when Columbus felt he was approaching land on his first voyage west in 1492, sailors on the *Niña, Pinta*, and *Santa María* fought each other in scrambling to the **crow's nest** to be the first to glimpse land just over the horizon.

Formulating a Grand Idea

BY THE early 1480s, Columbus had acquired much practical knowledge of seafaring and of the distances between various Atlantic and African ports. However, in developing his grand idea that one could sail west from Europe to arrive in Asia, Columbus had to go further. He needed to seek academic support to develop and defend his scheme. Working with his brother Bartolomeo in Lisbon, Columbus spent considerable time poring over maps and works of geographical interest. He delved into books of astronomical wisdom. Columbus noted and underlined anything that could help him strengthen his idea. As he did this, Columbus formulated three critical assumptions that had to be acknowledged in order for his scheme to be accepted. As time would tell, all three turned out to be false.

First, Columbus needed to convince himself and others that there was only one ocean—the

Christopher Columbus plans his expedition to sail west to Asia.

Atlantic. Furthermore, that ocean had to be narrow.

Second, for a narrow Atlantic to exist, the world had to be relatively small, smaller certainly than Eratosthenes said it was. In addition, Asia needed to stretch as far as possible from west to east. In other words, Asia had to extend further away from Europe as one looked east, so that it was closer to Europe as one gazed west.

Finally, there could not be any large land-mass in the way as one sailed from Europe to Asia. Fortunately, the known world at the time of Columbus made no firm assumptions about an undiscovered continent.

In examining his sources, Columbus did not hesitate to see what he wanted to see. That is, he selected what information supported his growing belief that he could get to Asia in a relatively short time by sailing west, out into the Atlantic. He rejected or ignored what didn't support his position. In this, Columbus was no different than most others in trying to make a case.

Claudius Ptolemy (pronounced with the "P" silent) was a Greco-Egyptian born in 100 AD. His works on geography were rediscovered by Western scholars in the early 15th century. In reading Ptolemy, Columbus learned of two convictions that bolstered his later arguments. One, Ptolemy said the known world extended in one continuous landmass from the western edge of Europe to the easternmost limit of Asia. It did this for 180 degrees of longitude—halfway around the planet. Two, Ptolemy rejected Eratosthenes, deciding instead that the world was 30 percent smaller. Both ideas were music to Columbus's ears.

When Columbus next turned to the writings of Marco Polo, the late-13th-century European who spent close to 24 years in Asia, he gained further support. Polo, Columbus concluded, had traveled a lot farther east than Ptolemy's Asia extended. In other words, there was more land going east and thus less ocean to cross while traveling west. Furthermore, Marco Polo placed Cipangu (Japan), an island it is doubtful he ever visited, 1,500 miles east of China. The distance is actually less than 500 miles. Thus Asia would be even further west-to-east, and if a **mariner** sailed from Europe to

Marco Polo's journey from Venice to China.

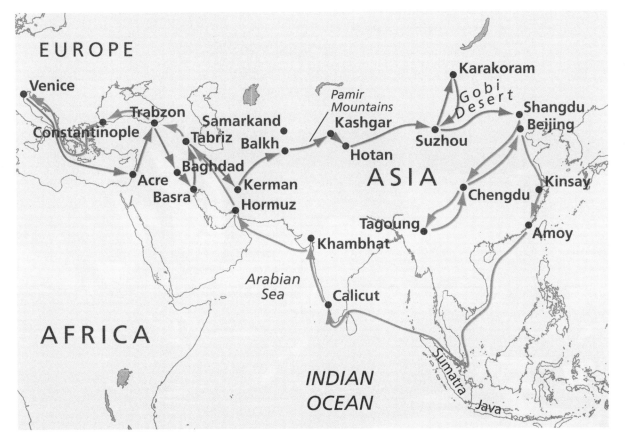

Asia, he could hit Cipangu long before going on to Cathay (northern China).

When one adds to these estimates of distance the claims of Marinus of Tyre (the rediscovered first-century **cartographer**), no doubt Columbus became even more excited. Marinus stretched Ptolemy's degree mark to 225 degrees, leaving just 135 degrees of ocean to transverse.

Columbus also turned to the highly respected Paolo dal Pozzo Toscanelli, a 15th-century Florentine astronomer with whom he corresponded, to seal his convictions. Independent

A portrait of 15th-century Italian scholar Paolo dal Pozzo Toscanelli. Thinkstock 125176238 (collection: Dorling Kindersley RF)

MAKE AN ANCIENT GLOBE

BEFORE THE voyages of Columbus and other explorers of his time, many knowledgeable Europeans thought that the world consisted of one continuous landmass surrounded by one huge ocean. The Greek mathematician Eratosthenes (256–195 BC) believed that this landmass amounted to only one-third the circumference of the earth. The inhabited world, in his view, was made up of three connected continents: Europa, Asia, and Africa. The geography of Europa was relatively well known, with Africa less so, and Asia least of all. Eratosthenes's world looked something like what is depicted in the accompanying drawing.

In this activity, you will create a globe that represents the world as it was thought to be in the time of Eratosthenes.

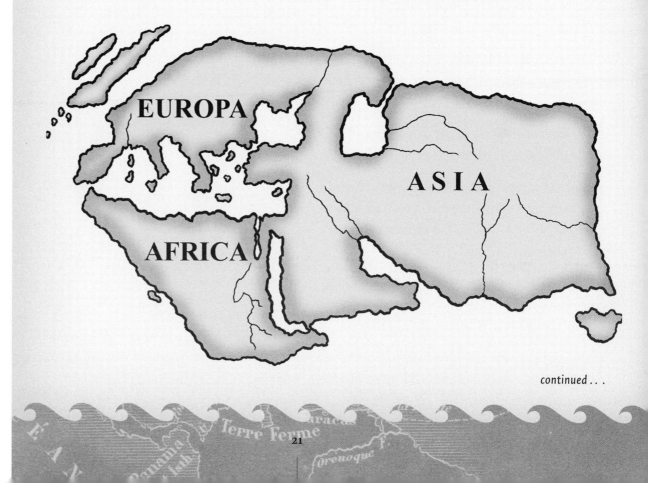

continued . . .

Materials

+ Round balloon
+ Nonstick cooking spray
+ Scissors
+ Newspaper
+ Mixing bowl
+ 1 cup flour
+ 1½ cups water
+ 1 tablespoon salt
+ ¼ cup white glue
+ Bowl to be used as stand for balloon
+ Tissue paper
+ Paintbrushes
+ A set of acrylic paints
+ 2 wet washcloths to keep hands clean

1. Inflate a balloon to approximately 8 to 10 inches in diameter and tie closed. Apply nonstick cooking spray to balloon's surface.

2. Prepare lots of newspaper strips. They should be 2 inches wide and between 4 and 6 inches long.

3. Prepare papier-mâché paste, the glue that will bind the paper strips together. Thoroughly mix 1 cup flour, 1½ cups water, 1 tablespoon salt, and ¼ cup white glue in a bowl.

4. Place the balloon in another bowl, or similar object, to use as a base while applying the strips of newspaper.

5. Dip a strip of newspaper into the papier-mâché paste, remove excess paste, and then lay the coated strip over the balloon. Smooth the strip out. Remove excess paste with your fingers. Alternatively, you may want to coat the balloon with a thin layer of papier-mâché paste and then lay strips of newspapers on the paste.

6. Do not place the strips side by side. Instead, layer and crisscross the strips to create a solid grid. Cover the balloon with six layers of papier-mâché strips. Leave what you have done to dry for at least 24 hours.

7. Create a smooth finishing layer for your globe by applying two layers of tissue paper using the same method from steps 5 and 6. Let dry for another 24 hours.

8. Once the tissue paper has completely dried, paint the entire papier mâché globe using blue acrylic paint. Let the paint dry for at least 30 minutes.

BOWL

9. Photocopy the map at from the previous page. Enlarge if necessary. Cut around the perimeter of the landmass. Hold the cutout against the globe and trace the map's outline with a pencil. Fill in the details. The landmass should take up no more than one-third the surface of your globe, west to east, and almost all of it should be placed in the Northern Hemisphere, above the equator. The rest of the globe is water.

10. Paint landforms on the globe using brown, tan, green, and white acrylic paint. Use a modern globe or map as a guide to where mountains and valleys might be. Let your globe dry for at least 30 minutes.

11. Pop the balloon. If possible, remove the balloon. If you find the balloon is sticking to the inside of your globe, don't worry. Just leave it there.

Display your globe. It is sure to be a conversation piece.

of Columbus, Toscanelli came to the same conclusions as the navigator. The world was small. The Atlantic Ocean was narrow. And Asia was close to Europe, maybe less than 3,000 miles away. If so, one could sail from east to west in a matter of weeks. (The distance from Portugal to Cipangu is actually over 12,000 miles.)

Finally, Columbus found biblical sources that, in his view, supported his thinking. In Book 2 of Esdras, chapter 6, verse 42, it says, with regard to the earth, "six parts hast thou dried up." Meaning, six-sevenths of the globe is land. If only one-seventh is water, there couldn't be that much ocean to cross.

Thus, with his considerable practical experience as a seaman, plus his selected readings, Columbus now had what he needed to present a viable proposal. He just had to find a sponsor willing to listen.

Making His Case

IN SEEKING a backer, Columbus needed to look for royal support. It was not enough to find a group of merchants willing to invest in his Enterprise of the Indies, as it would be called. To acquire the prestige, status, and glory he felt due to him if he were to undertake the difficult journey ahead, Columbus required the backing of a sovereign, a king or queen who could confer appropriate titles and wealth upon him. The navigator made his desires clear to any would-be patron when he said, early on:

So that from thenceforth I should be entitled to call myself Don and should be High Admiral of the Ocean Sea and Viceroy and Governor in perpetuity [forever], of all the islands and mainland I might discover and gain, or that might thereafter be discovered and gained in the Ocean Sea, and that my elder son should succeed me and his heirs thenceforth, from generation to generation, forever and ever.

Illustrated map of ancient Japan (Cipangu).
Thinkstock 112706972 (collection: Dorling Kindersley RF)

Elements of medieval court life.

In exchange for such demands, Columbus promised the riches of Asia to any sovereign willing to pay his way and grant him nobility. Of Cipangu, his projected first stop, Columbus was quick to quote Marco Polo's description of the island, all the better to whet a hungry king's appetite:

They have the greatest abundance of gold, for the sources of it are without end.... The entire roof of the palace is covered with plates of gold.... The ceilings of the rooms are made of the same precious metal. Many of the rooms have tables of massive thick gold, and the windows are also decorated with gold.... Also to be found on this island are great numbers of pearls, which are slightly reddish in color, round, and very large; of the same value as white pearls, or even more valuable.... There are also quantities of precious stones.

Columbus had lived in Portugal for the past eight years, and so it was only natural that in seeking royal patronage, he turned first to João II, king of that Atlantic-facing country. Sometime in the fall of 1484, Columbus, now 33 years old, was granted an audience with King João, and he proceeded to make his case for sponsorship of a voyage west to reach Asia.

While we know little about Columbus's actual presentation to the king, it is safe to assume the mariner was forceful and articulate. Nonetheless, the plan was eventually rejected. Three factors, it seems, were at work in King João taking a pass on the enterprise.

There was Columbus's personality. According to one account, "The King, as he observed this *Christovão Colom* [Christopher Columbus] to be a big talker and boastful in setting forth his accomplishments, and full of fancy and imagination with his Isle Cipangu than certain whereof he spoke, gave him small credit."

Many in the court came to see Columbus as vain; a man prone to bragging endlessly. What was taken as arrogance could only hurt Columbus's cause.

Then there were the demands themselves. Titles and the like were not a major stumbling block. It cost King João little to grant them. But when Columbus set forth more concrete financial requirements, problems surfaced. In addition to the honors Columbus demanded, he expected one-tenth of all the income received by the king from all the silver, gold, pearls, precious stones, spices, and other profitable objects found in the new territories. To many at the king's court, it seemed that Columbus, an Italian foreigner to boot, wanted too much.

Personality and demands aside, it is clear that Columbus's Enterprise of the Indies, as presented to the king of Portugal in 1484, failed to gain traction for the simple reason that few felt it would work. Some doubted the very existence of an island such as Cipangu. Others made it clear that the world was much larger than Columbus claimed. No ship of its day, they insisted, could sail an ocean for 3,000 miles without early on running out of water, wood, and other provisions.

Nonetheless, King João did not reject Columbus outright. The king formed a commission consisting of three learned men. They spent days questioning the navigator about his plans.

While delaying his official reply to Columbus, King João secretly assigned a ship to check out the navigator's claims. A supply caravel attempted to sail west as Columbus proposed. It wasn't long before the ship limped back to Lisbon, its sails ripped and its masts broken. The survivors complained of impossible conditions, of tempests at sea too monstrous to relate. Clearly, sailing west to get to the east was foolhardy, if not impossible.

According to Ferdinand Columbus, the mariner's second son (and his first important biographer), the operation that King João sent out failed for want of competency. Writing decades after the event and without witnessing the occurrence himself, Ferdinand declared:

Lacking the knowledge, steadfastness and ability of the Admiral [Columbus], they wandered about on the sea for many days and returned to Cape Verde and thence to Lisbon, making fun of the enterprise and declaring that no land could be found in those waters. When he learned of this, the Admiral formed such a hatred for that city and nation that he resolved to depart for Castile with his little son Diego.

Ferdinand's accusation against King João may have been overstated. In truth, Columbus and the king departed with little hostility. King João's rejection of Columbus's plan was based more than anything else on the impossibility of sailing such a long distance in order to reach the Indies. Besides, Portuguese ships were making good progress working their way down the African coast. Better, it was felt, to devote limited resources to the rounding of Africa in getting to the riches of the East.

To Spain

LATE IN the summer of 1485, a disillusioned Columbus left Portugal to try his luck in Spain. The 34-year-old explorer was poverty stricken and unemployed—virtually penniless. Creditors were on his heels. When he arrived in the southern port town of Palos, Columbus had his five-year-old son, Diego, with him. Before having any chance of approaching the sovereigns of Spain, Columbus had more immediate concerns. He had to find food and lodging, and someone to school and look after Diego. The mariner was not in a good position.

Having heard that a Franciscan monastery, La Rábida, situated high on a bluff just out of Palos, might be willing to take him and his son in, Columbus and Diego set out on foot to inquire. The two hiked three miles along a dusty road to the place of refuge. When the door opened, Columbus pleaded for help, needing food for his fainting son. La Rábida was known to take in travelers free of charge. The future Admiral of the Ocean Sea would stay at La Rábida for five months. Diego would be there much longer.

On the very first evening at La Rábida, Columbus met with Friar Juan Perez, the guardian of the monastery. Perez became Columbus's spiritual mentor for life.

Seeing that Columbus was interested in cosmology (the study of the heavens), Friar Juan introduced the explorer to Friar Antonio de Marchena, a man said to be of great intelligence and a worthy astronomer. Friar Antonio quickly embraced Columbus's ideas about traveling west to get to the East. Furthermore, Friar Antonio promised to help Columbus find a sponsor.

Through Friar Antonio's connections, Columbus eventually met the first Duke of Medinaceli, Luis de La Cerda. The duke, with extensive commercial interests, not only endorsed Columbus's plan, he put the explorer up at his palatial estate and helped him with a **stipend** (payment) that lasted for a year and a half. Little Diego, meanwhile, stayed at La Rábida.

While the duke himself was prepared to sponsor Columbus in his scheme to reach the Indies by sailing west, he soon thought better of taking on the project alone. Finances were not the issue. Luis de La Cerda understood that such an endeavor required more than just money. Royal approval was necessary. After all, in addition to commercial considerations, the sovereignty of the lands visited would be an issue. There would undoubtedly be negotiations with Portugal. And the Pope in Rome would surely demand to be involved. Columbus had to make his case to the sovereigns themselves.

To that end, in January 1486, Columbus arrived at Córdoba, seeking an audience with Queen Isabella and King Ferdinand. Unfortunately, the two monarchs had left for Madrid. They were not expected back in Córdoba until late April. Columbus had to be patient.

It was at this time, while waiting to see the queen and king, when Columbus met a young woman named Beatriz Enríquez de Harana. Beatriz, at the time only 20 or 21 years old, became Columbus's mistress. She eventually gave birth to their son, Ferdinand, on August 15, 1488, out of wedlock.

Columbus never married Beatriz. She came from a family of carpenters and butchers, and her station in life was too far beneath Columbus's own to satisfy the always socially conscience mariner. Nonetheless, Columbus always behaved responsibly toward Beatriz. In one of his last memoranda to his firstborn son, Diego, Columbus reminded him to, "Take Beatriz Enríquez in your charge for love of me, as attentively as you would your own mother. See that she gets from you 10,000 *maravedís* a year, beyond her income from her meat business in Córdoba."

On May 1, 1486, Queen Isabella and King Ferdinand, having returned to Córdoba, agreed to see Columbus. The two sovereigns had married in 1469. In doing so, Isabella of Castile and Ferdinand of Aragon united modern Spain.

In presenting his plan to the sovereigns, Columbus obviously struck a chord with the queen. The two were of the same age and, evidently, thought alike. Although Isabella was impressed with Columbus's arguments, like King João II of Portugal, the queen turned the issue over to a commission of learned men. Headed by Friar Hernando de Talavera, her confessor, the commission deliberated for

✠ The Reconquista

The Reconquista, or Reconquest, refers to the nearly 800-year struggle the Christians of Spain waged against the Moors, or Muslims, who occupied the Iberian Peninsula from 711 to 1492 AD. It was only after the final battle, at Granada, that the sovereigns of a united Spain, King Ferdinand and Queen Isabella, were able to breathe easy and agree to sponsor Christopher Columbus on his voyage of discovery.

In the initial Muslim invasion of Spain in 711 AD, the Moorish forces were able to almost completely overrun Iberia in just seven years. As a result, Iberia (Al-Andalus) became the westernmost part of an immense Islamic Empire ruled by the Umayyad caliphs (Muslim heads of state) from Damascus to Syria.

The Umayyad dynasty was short-lived, however. In 750 AD it was overthrown by the Abbasids in a bloody uprising. The Abbasids had invited 80 Umayyad leaders to a dinner in Damascus. Before the first course was served, 79 were clubbed to death.

One individual managed to escape by jumping out a window. Abd al-Rahman I, only 19 at the time, swam across the Euphrates River and fled in disguise. In 755 AD, al-Rahman arrived in Spain, where he eventually established a new Muslim kingdom.

Al-Rahman was considered an enlightened ruler. Christianity and Judaism were tolerated faiths. Women were permitted to learn to read and write.

In the 11th century AD, the power of the Umayyad caliphs began to wane. At the same time, the Christians, who had been able to hold on to a small section of land in the Iberian north, began to fight back in earnest. Their most famous hero of the Reconquista was a leader named el Cid. Though he was not above switching sides from time to time, el Cid inspired his supporters to great efforts.

The forces of Ferdinand and Isabella finally conquered the last Islamic kingdom of Granada in 1492. Columbus was there to witness their triumph. Good thing, for had the victory not occurred, the soon-to-be Admiral of the Ocean Sea may never have sailed for Spain—certainly not in the eventful year of 1492.

what must have seemed to Columbus a lifetime. They probably concluded their examination of the navigator's plan in the spring of 1487. The Talavera Commission did not, however, publish its findings until 1490.

In early 1488, Columbus, growing frustrated and impatient, wrote to King João II, offering to return to Lisbon and reopen negotiations. The king agreed, and in December Columbus arrived at the Portuguese court.

Christopher Columbus at the royal court of Spain.

The explorer's timing couldn't have been worse. He showed up only to witness the triumphant return of Bartolomeu Dias from his voyage around South Africa's Cape of Good Hope, thus discovering an eastern route to the Indies. As a result, the Portuguese had no interest in sailing west to the riches of the East. Columbus, dejected once more, withdrew to Spain. After four years of pleading and waiting, the man from Genoa had little to show for his efforts in finding sponsorship.

Destiny

IN LATE 1492, the Talavera Commission made its report public. The news was not good. It added up to yet another rejection for Columbus—a resounding one. The commission presented six arguments against the mariner's plan:

One, a voyage to Asia required three years—a sailing trip impossible with available technology.

Two, the Atlantic Ocean is infinite. In addition, it is probably unnavigable.

Three, if a ship were to somehow reach the other side of the world, it could never get back.

Four, there is no other land out there because the greater part of the globe is covered with water.

Five, of the five zones existing in the world, only three are habitable.

Six, so long after the Creation, it was unlikely there existed unknown lands of any value.

Of course, it was the sovereigns who would make the final decision on whether to support Columbus. King Ferdinand was cool to the plan and the man—he simply did not like Columbus. Queen Isabella, on the other hand, was not quite prepared to slam the door shut. She gave Columbus hope that he might again be able to present his plan at a future date. At the moment, the Crown was in a last ditch effort to wrestle the Iberian Peninsula away from the Moors (Muslims). Success, after 700 years of effort, was almost at hand. Once victory was assured, perhaps the sovereigns might be able to concentrate on new ventures.

Columbus, once again, found himself waiting and waiting. Yet, in the fall of 1491, for reasons still unclear, the mariner was granted yet another audience with Queen Isabella. In fact, the queen sent Columbus a sum of 20,000 *maravedis* so that he could acquire proper clothing and hire a mule to transport himself.

It was at this time that Columbus presented his winning card. He had heard all the objections of the various commissions. But now Columbus chose, in one desperate effort, to explain to the sovereigns how he, and only he, knew the way to sail to Asia and back.

Christopher Columbus's coat of arms.
Thinkstock 125176707 (collection: Dorling Kindersley RF)

CREATE A COAT OF ARMS

IN CREATING a family coat of arms, you will be thinking about what your family values, while thinking about how to represent those ideas symbolically and artistically. It is an opportunity for great personal expression, one that Christopher Columbus took full advantage of when the sovereigns of Spain granted him nobility, and, along with it, the right to his own coat of arms.

A coat of arms is not just a pretty logo representing an individual, family, profession, or organization. On the contrary, having an attractive medieval coat of arms was not the purpose. Everything about a coat of arms is symbolic; it has a particular meaning. When someone who knows the meaning of its symbols looks at your coat of arms, they understand what it communicates about you and your family.

A coat of arms is made up of background colors and emblems. Colors have a particular meaning. For example, yellow or gold means generosity. White and silver show peace and sincerity. Black symbolizes grief. Blue stands for loyalty and truthfulness. Red indicates military fortitude. Green is the color of hope. And purple is the color of royalty.

Many emblems are animals with symbolic importance. The bear indicates protectiveness. The bee means industriousness. A camel denotes perseverance. The dog symbolizes loyalty. The dragon is the defender of treasure. A lion stands for courage. And a horse represents a readiness to serve.

Keep the above colors and emblems in mind as you design your family coat of arms. For further information on the history and design of a coat of arms, known as heraldry, check these websites:

www.storyboardtoys.com/gallery
/coat-of-arms-lesson-plan.htm
www.makeyourcoatofarms.com/app.asp
www.makeyourcoatofarms.com/
www.yourchildlearns.com/heraldry.htm

Materials

- ✠ Scratch paper
- ✠ Pencil
- ✠ Shield template
- ✠ Glue
- ✠ Poster board
- ✠ Scissors
- ✠ Colored pencils, crayons, or markers
- ✠ Construction paper; various colors
- ✠ Embellishments, such as beads, feathers, foam shapes, yarn, tiny trinkets

1. Spend some time thinking about what your coat of arms should say about your family, its ancestry and values, as well as the activities the family enjoys doing together. Jot your ideas down on scratch paper.

2. Photocopy the shield template provided on page 31, or draw your own. (You can make the shield any size and shape you like.) Paste the template to the poster board. Cut the shield out.

3. The shield can be left as is, or divided into two or four sections. In each field you can add a symbol or color.

4. Color in the shield. If you divided your shield into four fields, each field can be a different color. Remember, colors are symbolic.

5. Draw on construction or plain white paper various emblems that will be glued to the shield in given fields. If necessary, color your emblems with colored pencils, crayons, or markers.

6. In the banner at the bottom, put your family's name.

7. If you like, add some embellishments, such as beads, feathers, or tiny trinkets to the shield.

Your teacher may want you to stand up in class and present your coat of arms. It will be interesting to see how your fellow students interpret your coat of arms.

Taking advantage of what he understood about the prevailing easterly and westerly winds, the former in the South Atlantic, the latter in the North Atlantic, Columbus was sure, as no one else was, that he could sail out to Asia and return to Spain. Knowing the winds meant knowing how to navigate a round trip.

It was also at this time that Columbus made further demands with regard to titles and financial compensation. "I will not glo-rify Spain for nothing," the future Admiral intoned. "If the sovereigns will grant me appropriate titles and honors to found a noble family, and the means for my descendants to keep up their rank, well and good. If not, I will go to France."

Yet again his request was turned aside. This time it seemed final. In disgust, Columbus turned back to La Rábida, preparing to leave the country.

On January 2, 1492, Granada, held by the Moors for centuries, surrendered to the queen and king of Spain. The Reconquest, as it would be known, was at last complete.

In early February Columbus, astride a trusty mule, left La Rábida and, with his now 11-year-old son, Diego, headed for Cordoba. From there he planned to meet his brother Bartholomew in France. At the same moment, one of his court friends, Louis De Santangel, minister of the budget to King Ferdinand, rushed to see Queen Isabella. According to Ferdinand Columbus, Santangel addressed the queen with a plea that changed the course of world history:

He told her he was surprised that her Highness, who had always shown a resolute spirit in matters of great weight and consequence, should lack it now for an enterprise that offered so little risk yet could prove so great a service to

The shaded areas show the earth as known when Christopher Columbus sailed. Library of Congress, Geography and Map Division, Robertson's Geographic-Historical Series Illustrating the History of America and the United States: From 1492 to the Present g3701sm.gct077

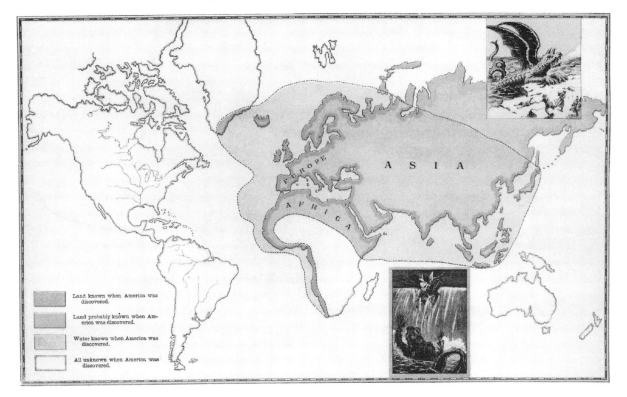

God and the exaltation of His Church, not to speak of the very great increase and glory of her realms and kingdoms. The enterprise, moreover, was of such nature that if any other ruler should accomplish what the Admiral offered to do, it would be a great injury to her estate and a cause of just reproach by friends and of censure by her enemies.

Santangel then suggested that if money was a problem, he would undertake financing the enterprise himself. Though the queen offered to put up her jewels as collateral (as a guarantee), Santangel assured her that was not necessary. Nor did she need to pawn her diamonds, sapphires, and other jewels.

Isabella, obviously impressed with Santangel's arguments, immediately ordered that a messenger ride to catch Columbus. The dejected but defiant sailor was already on his slow, plodding way to Cordoba. Overtaken at the village of Pinos-Puente, Columbus was halted, turned around, and returned to the queen. As more than one historian has pointed out, the voyage to the New World began on the back of a mule.

✚ Articles of Agreement (Capitulations)

It took nearly three months of intense negotiation between representatives of Columbus and the Spanish Crown to hammer out an agreement as to just what the man from Genoa would receive for undertaking the dangerous voyage ahead. The Articles of Agreement, also known as the Capitulations, assigned economic rights and jurisdictional or administrative rights to Columbus in his voyage. Essentially, there were five articles:

(1) Their Highnesses appoint the said Don Cristóbal Colón [Christopher Columbus] their Admiral in and over all islands and mainlands "which shall be discovered or acquired by his labor and industry."

(2) The said Don Cristóbal is appointed Viceroy and Governor-General over all such mainlands and islands as he shall discover or acquire in the said seas, and he may nominate three candidates for each office, from which the sovereigns will select one.

(3) He shall take and keep a tenth of all gold, silver, pearls, gems, spices, and other merchandise produced or obtained by barter and mining within the limits of these domains, free of taxes.

(4) Any case involving such merchandise or products will be adjudicated by him or his deputy, as Admiral.

(5) He is given the option of paying an eighth part of the total expense of any ship sailing to these new possessions, and taking an eighth of the profits.

In addition to the list above, Columbus was "Empowered henceforward to call and entitle yourself Don Cristóbal Colón, and his heirs and successors forever may be so entitled, and enjoy the offices of Admiral of the Ocean Sea, Viceroy and Governor of the said islands and mainland."

NORTH AMERICA

Atlantic Ocean

Gulf of Mexico

BAHAMAS

FROM SPAIN

TO SPAIN

— Tropic of Cancer —

Straits of Florida

CUBA

Caribbean Sea

HISPANIOLA

CENTRAL AMERICA

Pacific Ocean

COLUMBUS'S
FIRST VOYAGE

SOUTH AMERICA

30N

25N

20N

15N

10N

5N

95W

90W

85W

80W

75W

70W

65W

60W

~ 3 ~

A Voyage of Discovery

IT TOOK 10 WEEKS for Columbus to acquire ships, outfit them, fill them with a year's worth of supplies, and find crews to sail them. A myth has grown suggesting that Columbus's three vessels, the *Niña*, *Pinta*, and *Santa María*, were useless, leaky "tubs," "crates," or "cockleshells" unfit for Atlantic voyaging. It is said that their crews consisted of convicts and harbor riffraff. And it was said that the sovereigns of Spain had so little faith in the voyage to be undertaken, they believed Columbus and his crew would never be seen again. Why waste money on good, well-equipped ships and equally good Christians to sail them?

Such was not the case. All three ships were skillfully built, rigged, equipped, and manned. Columbus himself wrote that the vessels were "well suited for the enterprise at hand."

The *Niña* was the smallest. It was a caravel, a vessel of around 60 tons and 70 feet long. The *Pinta*, also a caravel, may have been a bit larger, 73 to 75 feet in length, but still only 60 tons. The *Santa María*, Columbus's flagship, was a **carrack**. It was the largest of the three ships to sail. The *Santa María* probably checked in at 100-plus tons, with a length of 82 feet.

Ninety seamen shipped out with the Admiral. In gathering a crew, Columbus was aided by a royal order suspending all civil and criminal charges against anyone who signed up. Given this directive, some have assumed the crews were made up of desperate characters, criminals, and jailbirds. In truth, only four of the 90 could be seen as lawbreakers.

A half-hour before sunrise on August 3, 1492, Columbus's fleet sailed out of Palos, Spain. The squadron was bound for the Spanish-held Canary Islands, 1,000 miles to the south and 100-plus miles off the West Coast of Africa. After refitting and resupplying, the Admiral, 41 years old, set sail on September 6, west into the Green Sea of Darkness.

Every day that the tiny vessels sailed, they traveled further from the known and deeper

Christopher Columbus's ships depart Palos, Spain, on August 3, 1492.

Thinkstock 149614796 (collection: Universal Images)

into the unknown. During the first days, the easterly winds blew with force. Progress was good. On September 17, Columbus recorded he had traveled 150 miles.

At least that's what one of his logbooks said. In truth, Columbus kept two logs in recording distances traveled. One, containing the accurate reckoning, he kept to himself. The other, the phony log, he showed to the crew. The crew log indicated fewer miles traveled. Columbus didn't want his men to complain about being far from home. In reality, because Columbus overestimated distances, the phony record ended up being closer to the truth than the accurate one.

It was at this time that the fleet entered a huge oval of ocean known as the Sargasso Sea. For hundreds of miles, the water is filled with **sargassum**, or **gulfweed**, a green plant that floats on the surface. While the weed does the ships no harm, it grows in a part of the Atlantic in which the winds, at times, die down to almost nothing. The ships' crews became alarmed. They were less concerned that there would be little wind to take them forward, and more distressed that there might be none to take them home.

As the voyagers entered their third week at sea, farther from shore than any had ever been, they at last began to see land-nesting seabirds. Columbus and his men became hopeful.

TAKE NAUTICAL MEASUREMENTS

THERE WERE five units of measure widely used by seamen during the Age of Exploration. All are still used today.

The **nautical mile** is 6,076 feet. It is used as the unit of measurement by all nations for air and sea travel. The nautical mile is based on the circumference (i.e. perimeter) of the planet earth. You can divide the earth's circumference into 360 degrees, and then divide each degree into 60 "minutes." Each minute of arc on the earth is equal to one nautical mile.

The **statute mile** is 5,280 feet. It is referred to as the land mile, to distinguish it from the nautical mile.

The **league** was originally intended to represent the distance a person could walk in an hour. In many cases it was equal to three statute miles. At sea, a league is considered to be three nautical miles and is usually used to express depth.

The **fathom** was traditionally considered the distance between the fingertips of a person's outstretched arms. It is assumed to be six feet.

The **knot** is a unit of speed. If you travel at a speed of one nautical mile per hour, you are traveling at a speed of one knot.

It is often necessary to convert one unit of measurement to another. For example, if you are given a distance in nautical miles, you may want to know how far it is in statute miles. You may also want to do the reverse. Let's see how to measure distances in nautical miles on a globe, and then convert that distance to statute miles.

Materials
+ Globe of the earth (the legend should show distance in nautical miles)
+ A few sheets of white paper: 8½ by 11 inches
+ Pencil
+ Calculator

1. Make a paper scale that measures nautical miles. First, find the legend on the globe, and, using the edge of a piece of paper, mark off the distance in nautical miles. A typical globe might show a line representing a distance of 500 nautical miles.

continued . . .

2. Next, using the scale you have just made as a guideline, prepare a longer scale on the long, 11-inch edge of another piece of paper. Mark each line, starting with 500, then 1,000, then 1,500, and so on, depending on what your globe shows. You now have a paper scale that is graduated in nautical miles.

3. Using your paper scale, measure the distance between Lisbon, Portugal, and the eastern edge of Hispaniola (the Dominican Republic, in the West Indies). You should get something close to 3,100 nautical miles.

Take a few more measurements.

1a. What is the distance between Praia in the Cape Verde Islands and Trinidad in the West Indies?

2a. What is the distance between Istanbul, Turkey, and the Strait of Gibraltar?

3a. What is the distance from Lisbon, Portugal, to Ireland?

4a. What is the direct distance from Gambia to Cape Town, South Africa?

5a. What is the distance from Tokyo, Japan, to Singapore?

What if you wanted to know how many statute miles there are in the nautical miles you just measured? Since there are 1.1508 nautical miles in a statute mile, you simply multiply the distance in nautical miles by 1.1508. For example, if the distance from Lisbon, Portugal, to Hispaniola is 3,100 nautical miles, you multiply that figure by 1.1508. Your answer (when rounded to the nearest whole number) is 3,567 statute miles.

Now, convert the nautical miles you measured in problems 1a through 5a to statute miles. Record your answers and number them 1b, 2b, 3b, 4b, and 5b.

Remembering that a league us equal to 3 nautical miles, figure out how many leagues you traveled in the distances measured in problems 1a–5a. Record these answers and number them 1c, 2c, 3c, 4c, and 5c. Check your answers below.

ANSWERS:

1a. 2,000 nautical miles	1b. 2,300 statute miles	1c. 666 leagues
2a. 1,500 nautical miles	2b. 1,725 statute miles	2c. 500 leagues
3a. 750 nautical miles	3b. 860 statute miles	3c. 250 leagues
4a. 3,250 nautical miles	4b. 3,750 statute miles	4c. 1,000 leagues
5a. 2,750 nautical miles	5b. 3,150 statute miles	5c. 900 leagues

Nonetheless, as September turned to October, and the days passed without sight of land, the seamen became agitated, frightened, and up for a fight. Mutiny, especially on the *Santa María*, was in the air.

In response, on October 10 Columbus made his do-or-die declaration. The Admiral promised he would turn back in three days, maximum, if no land was sighted. Then, on October 12, at 2 AM, the cry went out, "*Terra! Terra!*" (Land! Land!). At daybreak, the 90 men of the Enterprise of the Indies strained to behold an island six miles away.

Island Hopping in Paradise

THERE WERE people on this island. And as far as Columbus and his men could see, they were all naked.

Upon landing, Columbus, along with officers and a few crew members, took possession of the island for the sovereigns of Spain. The Admiral was richly attired in scarlet, befitting a **viceroy**. He fell to his knees, kissed the ground, and thanked God for his good fortune. Columbus named the island San Salvador, in honor of the blessed Lord.

The Admiral recorded that the people he encountered were fluent in speech, though he understood none of what they said. They were

Christopher Columbus faced with a possible mutiny on his first voyage, in 1492.
Thinkstock (photographer: Photos.com) 92822549 (collection: Photos.com)

Christopher Columbus sighting the New World. Library of Congress LC-USZ62-5339

friendly and bore no arms, except small spears with a fish tooth attached at one end. They had no iron. When Columbus showed one of them his sword, the man grabbed it by the blade and cut himself. He did not know what it was.

Wanting the natives to develop a friendly attitude toward the Spaniards, "because more could be gained that way than by force," Columbus gave red caps to some and beads to others. In turn, the natives gave all they had: parrots, balls of cotton thread, spears, and a dry leaf they held in great esteem (tobacco). Columbus insisted his men take nothing from the people without giving something in return. At least in the beginning, Columbus was thinking about trading, not raiding.

It was shortly after, however, that the Admiral revealed another side, one that did not bode well for the people he called Indians, in the belief that he had landed on one of the numerous islands east of India. "They aught to make good and skilled servants, for they repeat very quickly whatever we say to them," Columbus recorded. "I think they can easily be made Christians, for they seem to have no religion. If it pleases Our Lord, I will take six of them to Your Highnesses when I depart, in order that they may learn our language."

Christopher Columbus landing at San Salvador on October 12, 1492.
Library of Congress LC-USZ62-46115

The Admiral had landed in what is today known as the Bahamas. He spent the next two weeks island hopping, all the time commenting on how the last one visited was even more beautiful than the previous. The Indians he encountered were known as the Taino. They all spoke the same language, Arawak. Everywhere the Admiral went, the Taino assured him the little gold they wore in their noses could be found in abundance somewhere farther on. The place most mentioned was an island they called Colba. On October 24, Columbus headed southwest to Cuba.

Arriving on the northeast side of Cuba on October 28, Columbus once again marveled at the beauty of what he encountered. He wrote in his journal, "The island is filled with very beautiful mountains, although they are not long, only high.... They [the Indians] told me that the island is so large that they cannot circumnavigate it with their canoes in 20 days."

Two days later, on October 14, Columbus went even further, with the dark thought that the inhabitants of this new world could, perhaps, be enslaved. "These people" he noted, "are very unskilled in arms . . . with fifty men they could all be subjugated and made to do all that one wished." Though it would take more than 50 Spaniards to do it (and the Indians would prove to be less passive than he first supposed), in just a few short decades all of what Columbus said would come to pass.

Columbus spent five and a half weeks clawing his way along 200 miles of the northeast Cuban coast. In doing so, he communicated by sign with many Indians. They assured him that a mainland was just a few days' sail west. Columbus was now hearing what he wanted to hear. In the end, he came to believe, firmly, that Cuba was not an island, but part of that mainland—and the mainland was China.

Columbus's Ships

Of the three ships assigned to Columbus for his voyage west in 1492, *la Niña* ("The Girl") and *la Pinta* ("The Painted One") were caravels. The third, the *Santa Maria*, Columbus's flagship (the ship that carries the commander), was a carrack.

The caravel, developed in the mid-15th century by the Portuguese under the guidance of Prince Henry the Navigator, revolutionized exploration of the Atlantic Ocean. A typical caravel was a small, highly maneuverable sailing ship, with a tonnage of 50 to 160 tons and one to three masts. Its key development was the inclusion of one or more triangular sails, known as lateens. With such sails, the ship could sail well into the wind (windward). Furthermore, the **lateen** sail, when coupled with a square sail, gave the caravel speed. It could sail faster than any other ship of its day.

Being a relatively small ship, the caravel had a shallow **keel**. As a result, it could sail upriver. Columbus found this factor a decided advantage while exploring the larger, river-bearing islands of the Caribbean.

The caravel's main drawback was its limited capacity for cargo and crew. Still, its advantages in speed and maneuverability outweighed this one shortcoming.

The *Santa Maria* was not a caravel, it was a carrack. As such, it was larger than the *Niña* and the *Pinta*. It could carry more cargo. Though the *Santa Maria* was slower than its two accompanying ships, it performed well for Columbus on his outward voyage. But after it ran aground on Hispaniola, the *Santa Maria* was not available for the homeward trip.

Christopher Columbus's three ships, the Niña, Pinta, *and* Santa Maria.

Thinkstock 125176217 (collection: Dorling Kindersley RF)

Make a Chip Log

CHRISTOPHER COLUMBUS and other mariners of his day relied on dead reckoning to get from one point to another. **Dead reckoning** is a process of calculating one's current position based upon known speeds over elapsed time and course. To do so, one must determine speed with reasonable accuracy. The chip log made this possible.

The chip log, a crude speedometer, consists of a light line (rope) knotted at regular intervals and weighted to drag in the water. The weighted end is tossed overboard at the ship's stern. The **pilot** then counts the knots that are let out of the ship during a specific time period. From the data, the pilot determines the vessel's speed.

In this activity, you establish your speed in miles per hour by walking or jogging. In doing so, you are doing what a ship's pilot did in determining a ship's speed. (Your walking symbolizes the vessel moving forward.) Here is an example of how you calculate speed:

Say you traveled 2,000 feet in three minutes. If you want to calculate how fast you have traveled in miles per hour, first you want to determine what percentage of a mile you have traveled. If you divide 5,280 (the number of feet in a mile) into 2,000, you will get 0.378, or, rounded off, 38

percent of a mile. Next, you want to determine what percentage of an hour is three minutes. If you divide 60 minutes (the number of minutes in an hour) into three, you will get 0.05, or 5 percent of an hour. Finally, divide 0.05 into 0.38. When you do the math, you should get 7.6, which is your speed in miles per hour.

Materials
✛ Rope, 100 to 200 feet long
✛ Stopwatch
✛ Calculator
✛ Pencil and paper to record and compute speed

1. Take your length of rope and knot it once every 5 feet. The longer your rope, the more time it will take to do this.

2. Tie a weighted object to one end of the rope.

3. Drop the weighted end of the rope on the ground, while starting your timer. Walk away from the weighted end of the rope as you let out the line. When you reach the end of the rope, stop the timer. Count the number of knots you see laid out and multiply that number by five. You now know the distance traveled and from the stopwatch, the elapsed time.

4. Let's say you traveled 35 feet in 12 seconds. Dividing 5,280 into 35 gives you 0.0066, or 0.66 percent of a mile. Dividing 3,600 (the number of seconds in an hour) into 12 gives you 0.0033, or 0.33 percent of an hour. Now divide 0.0033 into 0.0066. You should get a speed of 2 miles per hour.

5. Repeat Step 3 above while either traveling faster or going farther using a longer piece of rope. What are your results? Try determining speed a few more times. Record your results.

The ability to determine one's approximate speed at sea was a major aid to exploration. It allowed a mariner to know, with some, though not great, accuracy, a ship's east/west position.

Finding the sailing along the Cuban coast difficult, and not seeing an ounce of gold, on December 5 the navigator left Cuba and headed southeast by east to Hispaniola (present-day Haiti and Dominican Republic), where he was sure there would be gold mines to exploit.

Shipwreck

ONLY TWO ships touched base at Hispaniola, the *Santa María* and the *Niña*. On November 22, the *Pinta* had simply sailed away from the others, unannounced and against orders, to explore the island of Babeque (Great Iguana). Its captain, Martin Alonso Pinzón, would search for gold on his own.

For the next 18 days, Columbus worked his way east along the northern coast of Hispaniola, an island he later told the queen of Spain was larger than her own country. On December 17, while exploring inland, Columbus met the most powerful **cacique** (king) who ruled northern Hispaniola, a man named Guacanagari. In an exchange of gifts, Guacanagari give the Admiral a mask with the ears, tongue, and nose of solid gold. Where, Columbus wondered, had this gold come from? Was it mined on this large island that he was now exploring?

Columbus was quick to note that the people he encountered were peaceful and content. To

Christopher Columbus shouting at the **Pinta** *as it sails off.* Thinkstock 125176211 (collection: Dorling Kindersley RF)

✠ Dogs That Do Not Bark

Wherever Columbus and his men went in the Caribbean, they commented on encountering dogs that did not bark. These were small hound dogs that the Tainos domesticated and kept for food. They could grunt but not bark during infancy and the first few years of their lives. Eskimo dogs today do not bark until they learn to do so from their parents.

According to Michele de Cuneo, a man who accompanied Columbus on his second voyage, the roasted barkless dog tasted "none too good." Others report that what was known to the Spaniards as *perros mundos* became extinct because the Europeans liked to eat them only too well. In any case, the barkless dog of the Caribbean no longer exists.

him and his men, it seemed the lucky Europeans had fallen upon a blissful paradise, one filled with beautiful harbors and peaceful, surprisingly unclothed men and women:

These people have no spears, arrows, or any other arms, nor have the other inhabitants of this island, which I believe to be very large. They are as naked as their mothers gave them birth men as well as women—unlike the people of Juana [Cuba] and the other islands, where the women wore in front pieces of cotton, something like men's drawers, with which they cover their private parts, especially after the age of 12. But here neither young nor old wore anything.

On Christmas Eve, Columbus and his two ships were off what would be called Cape Haitien Bay. The vessels were almost motionless in a sea as calm as a sheet of glass. Everyone was exhausted. The Admiral and his men retired for the evening.

A short time before midnight, the *Santa Maria*'s helmsman, the only member of the crew still up, awoke the grommet (a ship's boy), whose duty it was to turn the *ampolleta* (half-hour glass) as soon as the sand ran out. The helmsman, wanting to sleep himself, gave the grommet the huge, difficult-to-handle tiller, something Columbus had forbidden a boy to take under any circumstances. The only one

now awake on the *Santa Maria* was a **grommet** in charge of steering the ship.

Within minutes, the *Santa Maria* gently, and at first, noiselessly, floated on to a coral reef. As the boy heard the rudder scrape the reef, he shouted for help. Columbus was the first on deck. Men, violently awoken, scurried about in complete confusion. The *Santa Maria* had **run aground**.

As each swell of the sea lifted the flagship up, when the water retreated, the *Santa Maria* was dashed down on the reef. Seams in the ship's hull sprang open.

Columbus ordered the mainmast cut down, the better to lighten the vessel. It did no good. The *Santa Maria* was abandoned on the reef; the crew transferred to the *Niña*. In the morning a salvage operation began.

With help from Guacanagari and his men, the *Santa Maria* was stripped of all its stores. From time to time, Guacanagari sent his relatives to console the weeping Admiral of the Ocean Sea. To now see the man the Indians assumed had come from heaven, crying like a baby, must have been as confusing as it was shocking.

It wasn't long before Columbus, a man who saw divine intervention at every turn, concluded that, "Our Lord had caused me to run aground at this place so that I might establish a settlement here." To Columbus, the shipwreck was a blessing in disguise. He used the wood from the *Santa María* to build a fort, the nucleus of a future colony. Columbus gave the new settlement the name of La Navidad, since its unintended founding occurred on Christmas Day.

There was no way all the Spaniards now stranded on Hispaniola could cram aboard the *Niña* for the return trip to Spain, particularly now that several Indians would be traveling to Spain as well. Columbus, therefore, selected 39 men, some of whom eagerly volunteered, to stay behind. He assured them he would return. When he did come back, Columbus declared, he expected to find a thriving community where the abandoned men were living in peace with the Indians and where much gold had been gathered from the yet-to-be discovered mines of Hispaniola.

Sailor steering a ship.
Thinkstock 84289847 (collection: Dorling Kindersley RF)

Homeward Passage

ON JANUARY 16, 1493, the *Niña* and the *Pinta* (the latter having returned, without finding any gold) sailed north by east toward the **westerlies**, at 32° north latitude, heading for Spain. This journey was the first homeward passage from mid-America to Europe.

For the next 26 days, the fleet experienced smooth sailing. Columbus chose his route home well; with westerly winds to fill the ships' sails, there were days when the squadron averaged 150 nautical miles. On February 6, Columbus made 200 miles, a feat even a modern yacht might have trouble repeating.

The easy sailing, however, ended abruptly on February 12. On this day there rose up such a storm in the wintry North Atlantic, there were times when it was feared both ships would sink. Indeed, the *Pinta* was again lost, this time due to the weather, not a captain's decision to desert. Though the crew of the *Niña* tried to hail the *Pinta*, all they could do is watch Pinzón and his crew drift further and further away.

Make a Half-Hour Glass

For Christopher Columbus and other mariners of the late 15th-century, the hourglass (actually, half-hour glass) was an indispensable timekeeper. Since a **watch** aboard ship lasted four hours, there were eight turns of the half-hour glass during a sailor's watch. When a half hour was up, a ship's boy turned the half-hour glass over and a new half-hour sequence began. At each turn, the boy shouted out the time.

Materials

+ 2 identical half-liter clear, plastic water bottles
+ Sharpened pencil
+ 1 piece card stock or cardboard (the back of a notepad works nicely)
+ Single-hole punch
+ Dry, extremely fine-grained sand (dry salt will also work)
+ Clear tape
+ Duct tape (or similar)
+ Scissors
+ Stopwatch

1. Remove the outer labels from your bottles. Drain the bottles of any liquid. The inside of your bottles must be completely dry. The best way to achieve this is to leave the bottles open in a dry, hot place. It may take up to 24 hours for all the moisture to be drawn out.

2. Trace the outline of a bottle opening on the cardboard. You are making a circle the diameter of the bottle opening. Cut out the circle. Punch a hole in the center of the cardboard circle using a standard hole punch.

3. Fill one bottle halfway up with sand (or salt).

4. Using clear tape, fasten the cardboard circle to the top of the bottle containing sand. Be sure the card circle seals well to the bottle.

5. Place the other bottle on top of the first one, with one opening facing the other. Use duct tape to secure both bottles together.

6. Turn the bottles such that the one with sand starts draining into the empty bottle. Using a stopwatch, determine the time it takes for all of the sand to drain from one bottle to the other.

7. Repeat Step 6 by turning the device over. Record again the time it takes for the sand to fully drain from the bottle. (You should be getting times of about two minutes.)

8. To lengthen the time, you need to reduce the size of the hole in the card disk. Take off the duct tape. Cut a ⅜-inch square piece of card stock or cardboard. Using a piece of clear tape, grab the square such that the tape is at an edge. Use the cardboard square to cover half the hole and tape it securely in place.

9. Repeat Steps 6 and 7 and record your results. Your time should have doubled to around four minutes.

10. To get your half-hour glass to actually measure close to one-half hour, you will need to constrict the hole even further. Experiment by moving the cardboard square so that only a small opening is available for the sand to sift through.

NOTE: If you make the hole too small, the sand will soon clog up the hole and your half-hour glass will stop functioning.

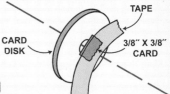

Once again, Columbus sought divine intervention. The Admiral and his men took a solemn vow that upon reaching the first land they would all proceed, wearing only their shirts, to a local church. By wearing just their shirts, no pants or shoes, the sailors would be clad in the proper penitential (regrets for one's misdeeds) garb. In doing so, the crew hoped to be forgiven their sins, allowing their souls to enter heaven.

It was at this time that Columbus, fearing he may never make it back to Spain, wrote out an account of his discoveries. He wrapped the letter in wax cloth, put it in a barrel, and threw it overboard and into the raging ocean.

On February 15, once again displaying amazing navigational skill, Columbus spotted land. He had found the Azores, a group of islands 800 miles west of Portugal and owned by that country.

Though Portugal and Spain were at this time at peace, Columbus was apprehensive about landing on Portuguese territory. Still, a meeting with officials seemed to go smoothly—at first. The Portuguese even aided Columbus in finding a priest to help him and his men carry out their vow of penitence. The Admiral sent half his crew, 10 men in all, to make the pilgrimage. He remained on board the *Niña* and went with a second group later.

The men in the first contingent removed their shoes and, clad only in shirts, took a boat to shore and from there proceeded to a tiny chapel. After beginning their prayers, they were rudely interrupted by Portuguese soldiers and taken prisoner. They were, literally, caught with their pants down.

Through careful negotiations, cool heads prevailed, and the men were released. On February 24, Columbus put to sea, hoping to reach Spain in a matter of days. Instead, with storms still raging, it was all Columbus could do to make it to Lisbon in Portugal. There, he was summoned to meet with King João II, the man who had turned down his Enterprise of the Indies almost a decade earlier.

While Columbus sat in King João II's presence, telling the king of all his adventures and what he had discovered, the sovereign of Portugal silently fumed. João II challenged two Indians in Columbus's group to rearrange beans on a flat table to show the positions of the islands they came from. Both, working separately, rearranged them in the same manner.

Some of King João II's advisers thought it best to eliminate Columbus then and there. They counseled the king that Columbus could easily be provoked, given his arrogant and overbearing personality, and in the resulting skirmish, be killed. Fortunately for the Admiral of the Ocean Sea, the king would have none of it. He sent Columbus on his way with good tidings.

On March 13, Columbus sailed out of Lisbon, bound for Palos, Spain. He arrived two days later—home from another world.

Celebration Time

WHILE STILL in Lisbon, Columbus wrote a detailed letter to the court in Spain and sent it by special courier. Upon arrival, the letter was quickly published, and news of the Admiral's discoveries spread rapidly throughout Spain, Portugal, and Italy.

The letter filled Europeans with wonder. There were rivers of gold, Columbus declared. Beautiful unspoiled lands existed for mile upon mile. Exotic birds filled the skies. Spices and cotton could easily be had. Columbus also stressed that the natives were passive. As a result, they could easily be converted to Christianity, he assured his readers.

The *Niña*, riding a flood tide, entered the harbor at Palos around midday on March 15. Its round-trip voyage had taken exactly 32 weeks.

A few hours later, the *Pinta*, with Martín Alonso Pinzón at the helm, sailed into Palos and berthed near the *Niña*. The *Pinta* had missed the Azores and thus the violent storm that nearly sank Columbus and his crew. The ship had sailed straight on to Spain, where

The triumph of Christopher Columbus.
Library of Congress LC-USZ62-12822

Pinzón landed at Bayona, a Spanish harbor just north of the Portuguese border.

From Bayona, Pinzón had immediately sent a letter to the sovereigns requesting an audience. The king and queen responded they preferred to speak first with the Columbus himself. Pinzón, devastated by the royal snub and suffering badly from the trip's ordeal, left for his country house near Palos. A few days later he died in bed.

Columbus now traveled over land, from Palos to Barcelona, where the sovereigns were holding court. His journey, according to legend, can only be described as a huge victory tour, a triumphant parade. As Columbus marched along, with near-naked Indians by his side, brightly colored parrots squawking in cages, and gold masks on display, crowds gathered to pay homage. Columbus gloried in the attention and public support.

When the Admiral of the Ocean Sea met with King Ferdinand and Queen Isabella, he was greeted as a conquering hero. They praised their seaman to no end. They made him a nobleman. They bestowed upon him a coat of arms. And, most important, though the sovereigns may have had questions as to just what it was that the Admiral had discovered, they quickly gave their approval to all he claimed. Indeed, Columbus no sooner left the royal presence than the king and queen began to talk enthusiastically of a second voyage.

But there were doubts. They came mainly from those who had never approved of the voyage in the first place.

Christopher Columbus explains his discoveries to Queen Isabella and King Ferdinand.
Library of Congress LC-SUZ62-3035

Clearly, it was within Columbus's interest to claim he had reached the Indies. If he had not, he could expect nothing from the sovereigns—no titles, no gold, no power. Columbus insisted to one and all that he had discovered islands "in" or "toward" the Indies. With a second voyage, he assured everyone, he could easily reach the larger island of Cipangu (Japan) and the mainland of Cathay.

Yet there were those who insisted that Columbus could not have touched even the outskirts of Asia. The world was too large for him to have made such a trip. To his detractors, all Columbus had done was encounter more Atlantic islands, more Canary Islands farther west. As history would prove, his critics were more right than wrong.

~ 4 ~

Indigenous Peoples

IN COLUMBUS'S LETTER TO Queen Isabella, written on his return to Spain, the Admiral of the Ocean Sea told the sovereign that Hispaniola (his proudest discovery) was larger than her own country. It is not. Hispaniola is about 29,000 square miles. Spain is over six times that size. Columbus sailed only a portion of Hispaniola's northern coast, but to so misjudge the extent of the Caribbean island was uncharacteristic of the Admiral.

Though Hispaniola was small in relation to Spain, the New World that Columbus had found proved to be unbelievably large compared to where he had come from. Columbus would never know the extent of the Western Hemisphere. He would not even admit to its existence. But what would come to be known as North, Central, and South America is, combined, over 16 million square miles. Europe, by contrast, is only one-fourth that area.

225 MILLION YEARS AGO

135 MILLION YEARS AGO

PRESENT DAY

Sequence of illustrations showing how the earth was changed from Pangaea, the crust moving with continents breaking apart, and how the world looks today.

The Americas are fully 76 percent the size of Eurasia (Europe and Asia combined). Simply put, the New World is a huge landmass.

At one time, the size differences between the various continents didn't matter. That's because they were all one large mass. Some 225 million years ago the world's entire territory was a single supercontinent, known as Pangaea. This land, in turn, was completely surrounded by a lone sea, Panthalassa.

Through geological upheavals, in which the earth's crust was torn away, Pangaea began to split apart 180 million years ago. Slowly, large land bodies drifted across the planet's surface. They became the continents we know today.

In addition to North, Central, and South America (all of which are joined), there arose the Caribbean Islands. Known as the Antilles, they are divided into two groups. The Greater Antilles are to the north and west. They are comprised of Cuba, Jamaica, and Hispaniola (today Haiti and the Dominican Republic). The Lesser Antilles, to the southeast, form an arc of numerous islands, beginning with Puerto Rico in the north and ending with Trinidad in the south, just off the Venezuelan coast. The Bahamas, where Columbus first landed, are generally not considered part of the Antilles.

The Greater Antilles are made of continental rock. The Lesser Antilles are mostly volca-nic or coral in origin. Columbus believed the Antilles were the outer islands of Asia, only a few hundred miles east of the Chinese mainland. The Admiral would take that belief to his grave.

Migrants

AS RECENTLY as 25,000 years ago there wasn't a human in the entire Western Hemisphere. Then, the ice formed. It grew in massive sheets, in some places a mile deep, covering the northern regions of the globe. This big freeze created the last great Ice Age. In locking up in glaciers millions of cubic miles of precipitation (rain) that would normally have gone into the oceans, the Ice Age dropped sea levels as much as 300 feet. As a result, land bridges surfaced, allowing people to move into areas previously uninhabited. One of those land crossings, known as the Beringia, connected what is today Siberia and Alaska.

During the Ice Age, Mongoloid peoples living in central East Asia followed buffalo and deer as the animals trekked farther north to new grazing grounds in Siberia. The herds drew the Mongoloids out of Asia, across the Beringia, into Alaska. As the ice of North America slowly melted, it opened an ice-free corridor between the Laurentide and Cordilleran ice sheets, in what is today northwestern Canada. Year by year, in fits and starts, the migrants came through, striking ever further east and south. Over the next thousand years or more, these Amerindians, as they are called, eventually settled in every part of North, Central, and South America, as well as in the Caribbean.

The Amerindians were at first hunters—effective ones. Working their way down through an unspoiled land, they found plenty of game to kill. The mammoth (an immense creature similar to but larger than an elephant) seems to have been a particularly desirable food source—"a great ambulatory (movable) meat locker," as one historian put it. Often the animals were herded en masse into gullies or entangling bogs. They were then sent to their end with dogs nipping at their feet.

More often, though, the mammoth was stalked as an individual. The hunter sought to get close enough to throw a spear into the animal's gut. "Then you just follow them around for a day or two until they keel over from blood loss or infection," archaeologist Charles Kay has said. "It's not what we think of as sporting, but it's very effective."

Never having encountered the new, efficient human hunters, it wasn't long before beasts such as the mammoth became extinct. The same was true for many other large mammals.

In effect, the new inhabitants of the Western Hemisphere were killing off their food supply. They had to turn to other means in addition to hunting to stay alive and flourish.

The new migrants needed to grow their own food. They had to become **horticulturalists**,

✝ *Mythical Islands in the Atlantic*

While the existence of islands in the distant waters of the Atlantic such as Iceland and Greenland were known at the time of Columbus, there were mythical islands thought to exist but later disproven. One such island was Antilia, or the Island of Seven Cities. It is from Antilia that the Greater and Lesser Antilles in the Caribbean are named.

According to a map printed in 1424, known as the Pizzigano Chart, Antilia was supposed to be located south of the so-called island of Brazil. It appears as a large rectangle, due west of the Azores. The island's story was described on a globe made by a navigator named Martin Behaim, in 1492:

In the Year 734, when the whole of Spain had been won by the heathen of Africa [the Moors], the above island Antilia, called Septe citade, was inhabited by an archbishop from Porto in Portugal, with six other bishops, and other Christians, men and women, who had fled thither from Spain, by ship, together with their cattle, belongings, and goods. In 1414 a ship from Spain got near to it without becoming endangered.

Along with Antilia, an island called Satanezes is often depicted on mid-15th-century charts. It, like Antilia, is shown as a large rectangle. Were these two islands supposed to represent the two big islands of the Caribbean, Cuba and Hispaniola? Or are they Java and Sumatra, in southeast Asia? Nothing can be said for certain. But it is interesting that some 15th-century mapmakers believed that two large islands were out there, far into the Atlantic.

people who planted fruits and vegetables. In time they evolved into full-fledged farmers.

With agriculture came settlement and huge population growth. It has been calculated that a population of 100 individuals, with a birth-rate of 3.4 percent, could explode to 10 million people in less than 400 years. By the time Christopher Columbus encountered New World inhabitants, they had swelled into hundreds of diverse cultures. The Western Hemisphere had become filled with people. Some of these Amerindians lived in complex, sophisticated societies that in many respects rivaled those in Europe.

Advanced Cultures

ONE SUCH complex society was the Maya. Two main Mesoamerican (Middle American) cultures (the other being the Aztecs) existed at this time. The Maya occupied the Yucatan

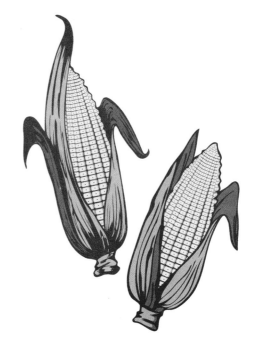

(ABOVE) *Corn ears, or maize.* *Thinkstock 96058790 (collection: Hemera)*
(LEFT) *Woolly mammoth.* Thinkstock (photographer: Photos.com) 92846290 (collection: Photos.com)

Peninsula and surrounding areas, such as Belize. The classic age of Mayan civilization ran from 300 AD to 1100 AD. When the Spanish arrived, Mayan strength and power were in decline.

The Maya were a sedentary (did not migrate from one place to another) people whose lives were based on maize agriculture. They constructed impressive stone architectural monuments and stepped pyramids. The Maya used two different calendars, one of which distinguished a solar year of 365 days. The Maya developed a pictographic and hieroglyphic written language using 850 stylized characters. As such, they were one of only five cultures around the world ever to independently generate a writing system—not an easy thing to do.

Yet, as advanced as the Maya were, they did not use metal tools or weapons. Nor did the Maya use the wheel. They did know of it, but for them it was confined to toys. Not having any domesticated animals large enough to pull a cart may have been one reason they did not make use of the wheel. But a human-powered wheelbarrow would have been quite useful. It never happened.

The Aztecs, the other major Mesoamerican civilization, were at their height at the time the Spanish appeared. They were ruled by an emperor, Montezuma. Their capital city,

CONDUCT A BLANKET (SILENT) TRADE

BLANKET, OR silent trade, is a method by which traders who cannot speak each other's language can exchange goods without talking. In this activity, trade will take place between two groups: one, Spaniards, and two, Indians of the West Indies. Spaniards came to the West Indies with plenty of items to trade. Some objects, such as glass beads, hawk's bells (small brass bells), brass rings, and knitted caps, were brought along specifically as trade items. However, the Spaniards also had many items of a more practical use, such as nails, ropes, matches, and medicines that could be bartered as well.

The Indians of the West Indies had relatively little to offer in trade. Nonetheless, what they did have was of considerable value to the Spaniards. The Indians had food the Spaniards needed to survive.

Materials

✠ 2 groups, 3–4 people each
✠ Goods to trade (gather the actual objects or a representation of them, such as pictures of the objects found in magazines or books or that you draw yourself):

European goods: bolts, nails, ropes, leather, yarn, flags, pennants, muskets, matches, crossbows, arrows, swords, lances, medicines, copper cauldrons, cooking pots, candles, flint, lanterns, fishhooks, nets, paper, magnetic compasses, half-hour glasses, rulers, drums, tambourines, glass beads, hawk's bells, brass rings, caps, etc.

Indian goods: breads, fruits, roots, sweet potatoes, tomatoes, yams, peppers, pineapple, wood, fish, parrots, flamingos, carved statues, tobacco leaves, hammocks, cotton, gold, gold objects, canoes, etc.

Conduct a blanket trade:

1. No talking or sign language is to be used.

2. Indian group lays out a blanket and places on it various goods they want to trade.

3. Spanish group comes and lays out its blanket, with various goods they want to trade.

4. The Indian group then decides to either accept the trade by taking the goods from the Spanish group (and leaving its own goods), or withdraws, leaving the Spanish group to add to or change out items to create an equal value.

5. Trade ends when both groups accept what is being traded and withdraw.

A high-ranking Aztec nobleman.
Thinkstock 112706758 (collection: Dorling Kindersley RF)

Kukulcan Mayan pyramid. Thinkstock 147080975 (collection: iStockphoto)

Tenochtitlán, was built on an island in a lake in what is now Mexico City. In splendor and population, Tenochtitlán was said to rival Paris.

For all that magnificence, however, the Aztecs were a pessimistic people. They lived in fear of displeasing their gods. To strengthen those gods, they fed them—with the hearts and blood of captured warriors. The Aztecs believed that strong gods better protected them and preserved the Aztec Empire. In spite of their numerous accomplishments that merit our admiration, there is no getting around it; the Aztecs were an imperial people. At their peak, they conquered and subdued most everyone else in the Valley of Mexico. The Aztecs waged continuous war upon their neighbors; both to gather tribute in the form of food and to extract victims for human sacrifice. They hoped that tearing a man's heart out while he still breathed would appease the gods.

It is difficult to know just how extensive Aztec sacrifice was—Spanish accounts differ widely. One account placed the number at 80,400 over a four-day period. A lower figure puts the killing of captured warriors by sacrifice at 4,000 a day. Either way, it was a bloody process, all built on the fear of offending heavenly powers.

The Inca of Peru were the third major advanced civilization to prosper in the Western Hemisphere. Their empire covered almost all of South America west of the Andes Mountains. North to south, it stretched from Ecuador to northern Chile. Eastward the empire spread to the borders of the Amazonian rain forest. The Inca capital, Cuzco, in Peru, was situated 11,500 feet up in the Andes.

The Inca Empire was governed by a god-king known as the Lord Inca. The Incas believed their kings were actual gods. In return for loyalty to the Lord Inca, every member of the society was given what they needed.

Inca civilization was not as advanced as that of the Aztec or Maya in that it did not have either an alphabet or a numbering system. But the Inca did have an amazing network of roads, which kept the empire in tight communication. Here, one historian describes what it was like to travel Inca roads, many of which stretched out at an altitude of two or more miles:

The Inca maintained a road network of over 18,000 miles, with teams of runners capable, on favored routes, of covering 150 miles a day. Between Huarochiriand and Jauja they climbed passes 16,700 feet high. The way stations studded the system at altitudes of up to 13,000 feet. Here workers were rewarded with feasts and pain-numbing doses of maize beer. . . . The famous Huaca-cacha ("Holy Bridge") stretched 250 feet on cables thick as a man's body, high above the gorge of the Apurimac River at Curahasi.

Though Columbus never encountered the Maya, Aztec, or Inca, the conquistadors who followed soon after him did. The result was devastating to these proud cultures.

Incan winding road at Machu Picchu, in the Andes Mountains, Peru. Thinkstock 119240858 (collection: iStockphoto)

The Arawaks and the Caribs

THE ARC of Caribbean Islands that extends from Venezuela to Florida provided a convenient series of stepping stones for Amerindians migrating north out of South America. The first to island hop in that direction were the Arawaks. It was the Arawaks (a subtribe of which were the Taino) who Columbus encountered on his first voyage to the New World.

The Arawaks were agriculturists who grew just enough food to live on. Maize and sweet potatoes were their main crops, though they also grew **cassava** and **yautia**. The Arawaks fished using nets made of fibers, bones, hooks, and harpoons. The Arawaks also liked to eat turtles. Their method of catching the sea-based animal was quite clever. The Arawaks first captured a remora, a fish with a suction cup on its head. The Arawaks then tied a line to the fish's tail and let it dive for a turtle. The fish attached itself to the turtle's back with its sucker. The line was then pulled up, and the turtle thrown into the fisherman's canoe.

The Arawaks also ate ducks, parrots, and doves. When they hunted small animals, the Arawak used a barkless dog, called a *perros mudos* by the Spaniards. The Spanish later came to like the taste of *perros mudos*.

To the Spanish, the Arawaks were seen, at least in the beginning, as peaceful and generous. Columbus wrote:

They are so ingenuous and free with all they have, that no one would believe it who has not seen it . . . Of anything they possess, if it be asked of them, they never say no; on the contrary, they invite you to share it and show as much love as if their hearts went with it, and they are content with whatever trifle be given them, whether it be a thing of value or of petty worth.

Native peoples offered the Spaniards yams and sweet potatoes.

Thinkstock 1401622 (collection: iStockphoto)

The same cannot be said of those to follow the Arawaks out of South America, pushing them north into the Greater Antilles. These were the Caribs, from which the English word "cannibal" is derived. From cannibal, in turn, comes Caribbean.

According to historian Kim Johnson, the Caribs were falsely portrayed as eaters of human flesh. "Following hard on the heels of the Arawaks, they [the Caribs] had supposedly gobbled their way up the Caribbean archipelago, settling on each island like a swarm of locusts in a field, and only moving on when they had gorged themselves on every available Arawak. By the time of Columbus's arrival, the Caribs had eaten their way through the Lesser Antilles and already were licking their chops for the meat walking about in Puerto Rico."

Dr. Chanca was a physician on Columbus's first voyage. According to his account, one day the Spanish arrived on an island occupied by Caribs who had taken a number of Arawak prisoners. Dr. Chanca gives a vivid explanation of what the Arawak captives thought of the Caribs:

We inquired of the women who were prisoners of the inhabitants what sort of people these islanders were and they replied, Caribs. As soon as they learned that we abhor such kind of people because of their evil practice of eating

MAKE A MODEL CANOE

THE ARAWAK of the West Indies, as well as the Indians of Central America, used dugout and bark canoes in paddling to nearby islands and to fish offshore. The single dugout canoe, hollowed out from a large tree trunk, offered advantages over a simple raft. It had more buoyancy (ability to float) and paddling was much easier. However, such a canoe did have one unfortunate drawback—with a rounded cross section, it was easily capsized.

It is odd that no New World Indians ever seemed to have developed the outrigger canoe, either single or double. The Polynesians of the Pacific Islands had done so, perhaps as early as the time of Christ. Having such a canoe creates much greater stability.

Attaching outriggers (a projection with a float as seen below) to the hull of a canoe reduces roll. The canoe is much less likely to tip over.

In this activity, you make two different types of model canoes and determine which one is more stable.

Materials

✣ Plastic water bottle; half-liters (16.9 fluid ounces)
✣ Scissors
✣ 3 wooden dowels, 3/16 inches in diameter and 12 inches long
✣ Single-hole punch
✣ 4 feet of string
✣ Tub in which to float the canoes
✣ Water
✣ Handful of pennies
✣ Ruler

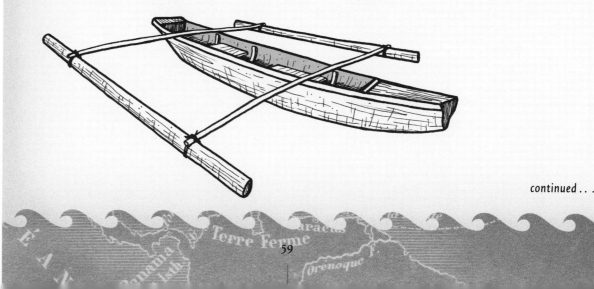

continued . . .

1. Cut your plastic bottle in half, lengthwise, using scissors. You now have two canoe hulls. Set one aside.

2. Using your scissors, cut two dowels 8 inches in length. Next cut two more dowels 6 inches in length.

3. Punch four holes in the plastic hull as pictured below. Two holes should be near the front of the bottle, across from each other. Two should be near the back of the bottle, also across from each other. The set of front and back holes should be approximately 4 inches apart.

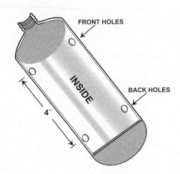

FRONT HOLES
INSIDE
BACK HOLES
4"

4. Insert the two 8-inch dowels through the set of holes, one in the front and one in the back. Center the dowels.

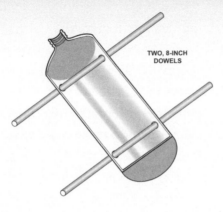

TWO, 8-INCH DOWELS

5. Cut four 12-inch strips of string.

6. Using a piece of string, tie a 6-inch dowel to the 8-inch dowel, as shown below.

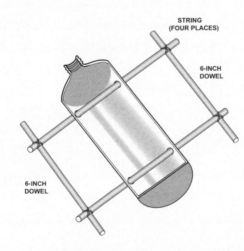

STRING (FOUR PLACES)
6-INCH DOWEL
6-INCH DOWEL

7. Repeat Step 6 three times to secure the two 6-inch dowel crosspieces.

8. Cut off the ends of each string.

9. Place both canoes in a tub of water.

10. As the canoes float, notice which one seems to be more stable, less likely to tip over.

11. Start gently placing pennies in the canoes: first a few pennies in one canoe, then switch to the other. Note again the stability of each canoe as the weight increases.

Both canoes will sink if too many pennies are placed in the hull. An outrigger canoe is not designed to prevent sinking. It is built to reduce the possibility of capsizing, or tipping over.

It's too bad the Arawaks did not have the outrigger canoe. Who knows how far from shore they would then have been able to travel, and what they would have discovered.

human flesh, they felt delighted. . . . They told us that the Carib men use them with such cruelty as would scarcely be believed; and that they eat the children which they bear them, only bringing up those whom they have by their native wives. Such of their male enemies as they can take away alive they bring here to their homes to make a feast of them and those who are killed in battle they eat up after the fighting is over.

In reality, there is no archaeological evidence of cannibalism in the Caribbean. Throughout the world, it is common for a given tribe to accuse their rivals of being cannibals. The Arawaks may have been seen as simple by the Spanish, but they weren't stupid. It was in their interest to tell Columbus and his men that enemies of the Arawaks were cannibals. By doing so, the moral anger of the Spanish would be aroused, and their antagonists would suffer the more for it.

Furthermore, it was also in the interest of the Spanish to accuse the Caribs of cannibalism. While Queen Isabella prohibited any Spaniard from capturing any Indians or doing them any harm, she made an exception of "a people called Cannibales... [who] waged war on Indians who are my vassals, capturing them to eat them as is their custom."

Queen Isabella further instructed that "they [the Caribs] may be captured and taken to these my Kingdoms and Domains and to other parts and places to be sold." Thus the incentive was there for the Spanish to discover as many "Canni-bales" as there were Indians. Slaves commanded a high price.

Before Columbus

CHRISTOPHER COLUMBUS was not the first European to set foot in the Western Hemisphere. It was 500 years before Columbus that the Norse from Norway landed in the New World. The Norse, however, took a decidedly different route west, traveling at Arctic and sub-Arctic latitudes (65° N), just south of the Arctic Circle.

Having reached the Faeroe Islands, northeast of England, in 800, the Norse colonized Iceland in 874. From Iceland they moved west to Greenland in 986. Finally, from Greenland, Norse sailors touched land in North America around 1000. They visited the continent in spurts from that date until 1350.

The Norse expedition that first landed in what is today Newfoundland was led by a man named Leif Eriksson. According to *Sagas of Icelanders*, Eriksson established a settlement at Vinland (Wineland), at a site known as L'Anse aux Meadows, on the northern tip of Newfoundland, in today's eastern Canada.

✝ John Cabot

John Cabot was actually a Venetian merchant named Giovanni Caboto. Under the sponsorship of King Henry VII of England, Cabot sailed west out into the Atlantic in May 1497. After a harrowing trip in his lone ship, the *Matthew*, the mariner arrived somewhere along the heavily forested coastline of Newfoundland or Labrador. Cabot returned to England in August and insisted to one and all that he had reached the far northern part of the Asian mainland.

A letter written within days of Cabot's return to England, by a fellow Venetian, sounds a lot like what was being said about Columbus upon his return to Spain:

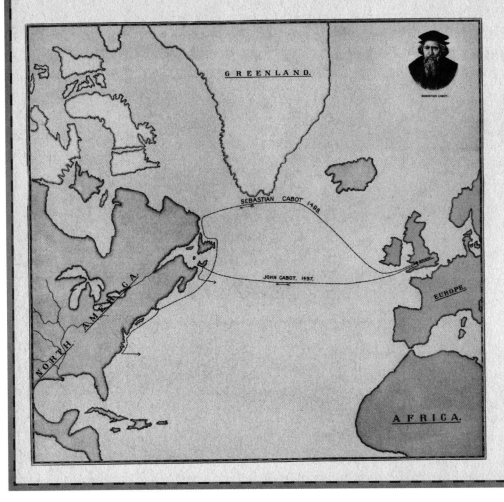

> *That Venetian of ours, who went with a small ship from Bristol [in England] to find new islands has come back and says he has discovered mainland 700 leagues away, which is the country of the Great Khan, and that he coasted it for 300 leagues and landed and did not see any person. . . . His name is Zuan Talbot [John Cabot], and he is called the Great Admiral, and vast honor is paid to him, and he goes dressed in silk, and these English run after him like mad.*

A map, printed in 1508, shows what John Cabot was reported to have discovered. On the same map, Cuba, Hispaniola, and other islands discovered by Columbus also appear.

In May 1498, Cabot was sent out on a second voyage. He was never heard from again. John Cabot's son, Sebastian, also became an explorer. In the year his father died, Sebastian made a lone voyage to the New World, and in later years he explored the North American coast in some detail.

The voyages of the Cabots.

Library of Congress, Geography and Map Division, Robertson's Geographic-Historical Series Illustrating the History of America and the United States: from 1492 to the Present g3701sm.gcto77

As the sagas pictured it, Eriksson heard a story of a merchant named Bjarni Herjólfsson who claimed to have sighted land west of Greenland. Eriksson sought out Herjólfsson and purchased his ship. He then gathered a crew of 35 men and sailed west from Greenland.

Eriksson first touched land at what is today Baffin Island. Two days later, sailing south, he landed in Labrador. From there he headed farther south, to the island of Newfoundland. It was here that he and his crew built a small settlement.

After wintering in Vinland, Eriksson returned to Greenland. He brought with him a cargo of timber and grapes.

Though the Norse are rightfully credited with being the first Europeans to land in what is today the Western Hemisphere, they were unable to sustain a permanent colony there. The colonial efforts failed because the latitudes were too high to sustain much food production. The Eskimos in the region knew only too well how to survive in the Arctic. But they were hunter-gatherers, not agriculturists.

It was left to Columbus and his crews, 500 years after the Norse contact with North America, to not only explore the new lands to the west but also to successfully settle them. To that end, the Admiral of the Ocean Sea led a second colonizing voyage to the New World, one fully intent on establishing a permanent presence.

Viking Leif Eriksson talking to men as his crew builds houses.
Thinkstock 98955345 (collection: Dorling Kindersley RF)

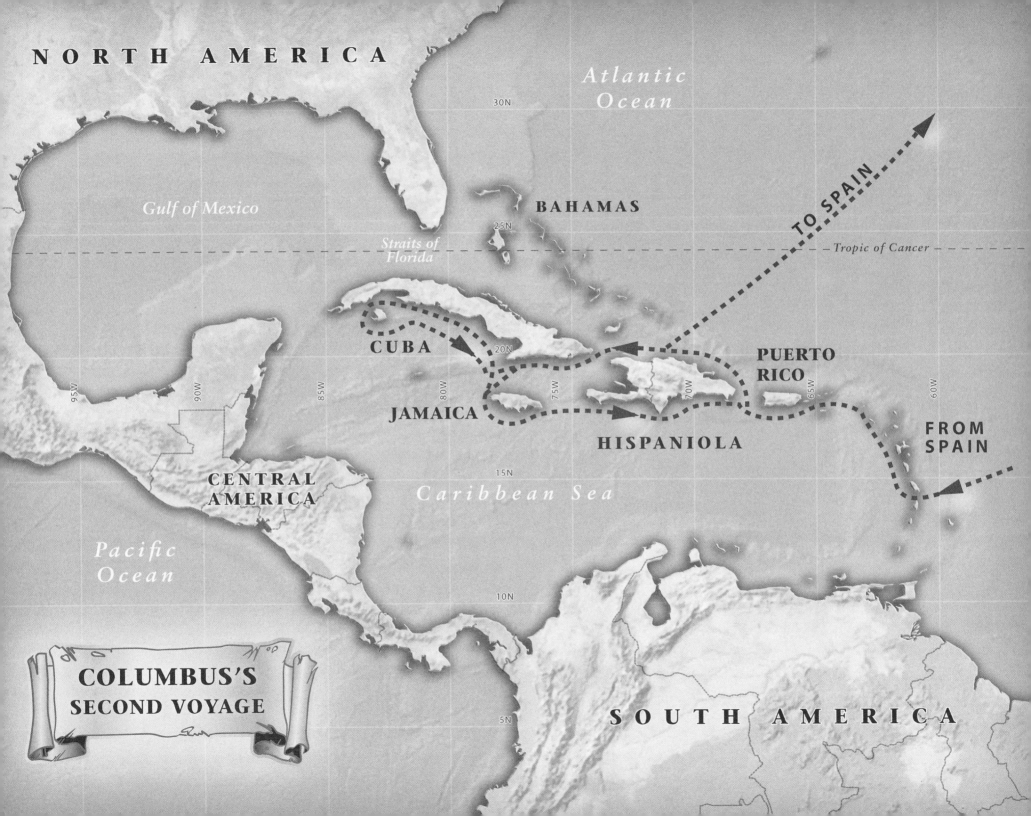

NORTH AMERICA

Atlantic Ocean

Gulf of Mexico

30N

BAHAMAS

25N

Straits of Florida

Tropic of Cancer

TO SPAIN

Pacific Ocean

CUBA

20N

JAMAICA

HISPANIOLA

PUERTO RICO

FROM SPAIN

CENTRAL AMERICA

Caribbean Sea

15N

95W 90W 85W 80W 75W 70W 65W 60W

10N

5N

SOUTH AMERICA

COLUMBUS'S SECOND VOYAGE

~ 5 ~

The Grand Fleet

COLUMBUS'S SECOND VOYAGE TO the Indies took five months of preparation. Given the armada to be launched (consisting of 17 ships carrying 1,200 seamen, colonists, soldiers, officials, and priests), it was no surprise it took time to put the enterprise together. In addition to men (no women yet), supplies were necessary to establish a colony. Pigs, cows, chickens, dogs, and, most impressively, two dozen horses, were boarded. Seeds and seedlings were packed. Furniture and building materials were stowed away. Everything necessary to establish a Spanish settlement in the New World was taken aboard.

Several hundred **hidalgos** were on the passenger list. These were men of nobility, disinclined to do actual work. Their aversion to any form of manual labor proved to be a serious drag on the new colony. Actually, most people on board weren't really colonists. They were adventurers who came to get rich from gold, a metal they expected to find practically laying around for the taking. Given all that Columbus had promised in bragging to the sovereigns of his wealthy Indies, it's understandable such individuals were attracted to the venture at hand.

The outbound **flotilla** left Cadiz on September 25, 1493. After the customary refitting stop in the Canaries, it took the fleet only 21 days to cross the Atlantic. On November 3, Columbus sighted an island in the Lesser Antilles. He named it Dominica. From there, the Admiral immediately sailed north, to an island he called Marie Galante. Upon landing, some sailors began scouting around. Tempted, they decided to taste an inviting-looking fruit. According to the squadron's chief physician, Dr. Chanca, who went ashore with them,

Christopher Columbus watches as a ship is being refitted for his second voyage.

Thinkstock 125176215 (collection: Dorling Kindersley RF)

66

"There were wild fruit [possibly the manzanillo] . . . which some rashly tried. But no sooner did they taste them than their faces swelled, growing so inflamed and painful that they almost went out of their minds. They cured themselves with cold compresses."

Columbus, anxious to reach La Navidad, left the Lesser Antilles and sailed north. He arrived off Hispaniola on November 25.

A shore party sent to survey the area found two dead, badly decomposed bodies. One of the men had his arms extended, his body in the form of a cross. On the following day, two more bodies were discovered. One had a beard.

The next day, when Columbus entered the La Navidad harbor, he fired two cannons, but there was no like response. Finally, two Indians approached Columbus's ship and asked to board. When the Admiral, through an interpreter, asked about the Spaniards, he was told a confusing story. Some, the Indians declared, had died of sickness. Others perished fighting among themselves. And still others had gone to the island's interior, where they took Indian wives.

In time what killed all 39 original inhabitants of La Navidad became clear. The Spaniards, with stern supervision lacking, quarreled over gold and, particularly, women. Not content with the two or three wives allowed by Guacanagari, the chief cacique of the region,

Three late-15th-century Christian priests. Thinkstock 112706805 (collection: Dorling Kindersley RF)

✠ Hidalgo

Hidalgo is a title in the Spanish nobility or gentry. Who was and was not entitled to call himself a hidalgo was strictly regulated. Hidalgos did not have any **fief** (or grant) or land. Though some were quite poor, they could join the civil service or the army. Their greatest advantage was their tax-exempt status. During the Middle Ages, the title of hidalgo was granted by the king of Castile. It was given as a reward for service done to the Crown.

Above all, a hidalgo was considered a gentleman. As such, he was expected to conduct himself in a civilized manner. Many, when placed in the Indies, did anything but. And their refusal to dig and get their fingernails dirty, something that had to be done if a new colony was to be established, was a serious shortcoming. Many hidalgos who came out with Columbus on his second voyage took the first ship home when the opportunity presented itself.

they began to pursue the Indians' wives and daughters. Led by a cacique named Gaonabo, revenge was quick in coming. The Spaniards who had not yet died from illness and infighting were wiped out, and their fort that was La Navidad was burned to the ground by the Arawaks.

Guacanagari, who was of tremendous aid to Columbus when the *Santa María* ran aground on the Admiral's first voyage, swore that he and his people had nothing to do with the tragedy at La Navidad. Guacanagari claimed he was wounded while attempting to fight off the attacking Gaonabo and his warriors.

Columbus was inclined to accept Guacanagari's story, though in doing so the Admiral angered many of his men who thought otherwise and wanted retribution. Abandoning the region, Columbus took his fleet 75 miles east, where, on December 8, 1493, he established a new colony, to be named Isabela. Clearly, the "gentle" Arawak were capable of vengeful acts.

La Navidad being burned down.
Thinkstock 125176210 (collection: Dorling Kindersley RF)

Escape to Cuba

THE SITE for Isabela seemed, at the beginning, a good choice. The colonists, eager to start the first true settlement in the New World, dug in and laid out a town. It was to have 200 reed and thatched huts, made from native growth. Yet it soon became apparent that Isabela was ill chosen. Columbus, knowledgeable about the sea, never seemed to understand what made for a good setting as a colonial outpost.

To begin with, Isabela had a poor harbor. It was open to the north and northwest, exposing everyone to winter winds. The harbor was so shallow that large ships had to anchor a half-mile out to sea. The soils were poor; they were not suited for European crops such as wheat, beans, onions, lettuce, and chickpeas. Little rain fell in the region. And, most important and frightening, Isabela, established in a mosquito-infested marsh, was a breeding ground for infectious diseases. It wasn't long before the colonists, in significant numbers, fell seriously ill.

Within a week of landing, 400 men took to their beds. Exposure to the elements may have been the first cause. Unappetizing native food that the colonists were never able to get used to did not help. And all the hard work required in building a colony, particularly in the tropics, added to the strain. This was not what the colonists had bargained for.

Even Columbus became sick. The Admiral was so ill, he was unable to keep a journal from December 11, 1493, to March 12, 1494.

Dissatisfaction quickly emerged. Most vocal among the malcontents were the hidalgos, for whom all the work and terrible living conditions were distasteful and depressing.

Furthermore, it became clear to Columbus that of the 17 ships that lay in the Isabela harbor, most would have to be sent home—and sooner rather than later. It was costly to keep vessels out in the Indies, doing nothing but standing by. There was not only the expense of paying the crews, there was also lost income since the ships would not be shipping goods to other parts of the world. In addition, the colony was desperate for resupply. Hopefully some of the ships would return within a few months. As a consequence, on February 2, 1494, Columbus placed Antonio de Torres in command of 12 ships that sailed for Spain. Columbus kept five ships for himself. Three small ones were used for coastal explorations, and the two large ships for storage. One of the smaller vessels was the ever-trustworthy *Niña*.

Desperate to get out to sea—to do what he loved best, explore and discover—Columbus now prepared to do just that. On April 30, 1494, the Admiral, with three ships, left for Cuba. He was determined to prove that what and then a few miles beyond, black as night. White chalk at the bottom in the first instance, and black sand in the second, proved to be the explanation for this odd phenomenon.

On June 12, Columbus, pushing west, reached a point where the southern coast of Cuba begins to swing southwest. It was here, only 50 miles from the westernmost end of the island, that his crews would go no further. Tired beyond endurance, they demanded that the Admiral return to Hispaniola. They had already taken a side trip that had resulted in the discovery of Jamaica island. What was to be gained by going farther?

Columbus, himself in less than good health, agreed to turn back—but only on one condition. In what has been seen by historians as a truly bizarre act, Columbus now demanded that every single individual aboard his three ships sign an oath declaring that Cuba was not an island, but part of the Asian mainland, perhaps the Malay Peninsula. It was no casual oath. A notary public was required to take down everybody's sworn statement. If, at a later date, anyone decided to recant, he would be fined 10,000 *maravedís* and have his tongue cut out.

It was thus that Columbus convinced himself, if not his men, that he was, indeed, in Asian waters. Cuba, to be sure, is an island, and a long way from the true Indies. The Admiral

Christopher Columbus presenting native people with gifts.

he was about to explore was a peninsula, and part of the Asian mainland.

The survey was time consuming; Columbus did not return to Isabela until August 20, 1494. Traveling west off the southern coast of Cuba proved to be slow sailing. The drudgery and tension of constantly fighting contrary winds and currents took its toll on the sailors. Still, there were flamingos to be seen as well as pilot fish that swam with sharks. And the crews were awestruck when the sea turned milky white of the Ocean Sea never accepted this fact, and he died believing the contrary.

Slaves for the Crown

COLUMBUS RETURNED to Hispaniola on August 20—but not to Isabela. Before reaching the colony on the north side of the island, the Admiral wanted to explore its southern coast. From there he had hoped to reach Puerto Rico, where the plan was to raid a Carib settlement and destroy their canoes so they would pose no danger to the Indians of Hispaniola. But in the channel between the two islands, Columbus collapsed from exhaustion. His son Ferdinand wrote:

From that point on, the Admiral ceased to record in his journal the day's sailing, nor does he tell how he returned to Isabela. He relates only that because of his great exertions, weakness, and scanty diet, he fell gravely ill. . . . He had a high fever and a drowsiness, so that he lost his sight, memory and all other senses. . . . This illness was caused by his great exertions on that voyage and the resulting exhaustion, for he sometimes went eight days with less than three hours' sleep. This would seem impossible did he not himself tell it in his writings.

MAKE A COMPASS

THE MAGNETIC compass is the most important navigational instrument ever invented. It consists of a magnetized needle that points north. By knowing where north is, one can use the compass to find other directions. Columbus made extensive use of the magnetic compass; you can make a simple one yourself.

Materials

✛ Sewing needle
✛ Magnet
✛ A few sheets of white paper
  (8½ by 11 inches)
✛ Scissors
✛ Water
✛ Small bowl (preferably transparent)
✛ Manufactured magnetic compass
✛ Round paper plate (10 to 12 inches in
  diameter and white on the bottom)
✛ Ruler
✛ Drawing compass
✛ Pencil
✛ Set of colored pencils or markers

First you will make the magnetic compass, then you will construct the compass rose (a circle divided into degrees to show direction).

MAKE THE MAGNETIC COMPASS

1. Scrape the dull end of the sewing needle across the magnet 100 times in order to magnetize the needle. Be sure to go in the same direction each time, otherwise the needle will not become magnetized.

2. Cut a small square of paper (try a 1½-inch square) from an 8½-by-11-inch piece of paper. Fill the bowl with water and place the small piece of paper on top.

3. Set the needle on top of the paper. Gently cause the paper to spin a bit. It is important that the needle be far away (at least 2 feet) from any metal and the magnet. If the paper gets stuck at the side of the bowl, nudge it gently toward the center.

4. Wait a few moments and your needle should be pointing north. To prove that it is, set the manufactured magnetic compass nearby, but still at least 2 feet away. Are both needles pointing in the same direction?

continued . . .

MAKE THE COMPASS ROSE

NOTE: You may want to practice steps 5 through 10 on a sheet of white paper before actually doing them on a paper plate.

5. Turn your paper plate over so the bottom faces up. Using a ruler, find the center of the paper plate and mark it. Using a drawing compass, inscribe a circle in the center equal in diameter to the bottom of your bowl. If you like, it might be easier to simply place the bowl of water on the plate and trace around the bottom of it.

6. To create a 16-point compass rose, you need to draw 16 lines coming from the center of the plate, each 22-1/2 degrees apart. To do this, you will bisect (divide in half) various angles.

7. Begin by drawing a vertical straight line though the center of your plate. This will be the north-south line. To bisect this line, to create an east-west line at a right angle (90 degrees) to the north-south line, use your drawing compass as shown in the first illustration above (step 7).

8. Bisect a line between north and east, as shown. Using your drawing compass, inscribe arcs through the plate's center, as shown in step 8. Draw the northeast–southwest line.

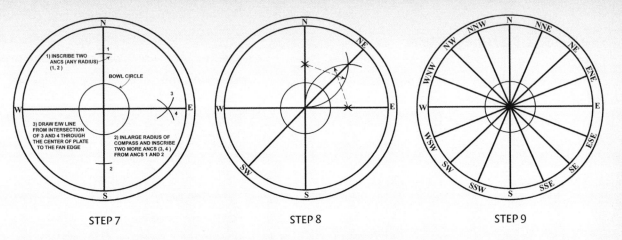

STEP 7   STEP 8   STEP 9

9. Keep bisecting lines until you have 16. Label the ends of your lines with north, north-northeast, northeast, etc., as shown in the last illustration above (step 9).

10. Now, using the four 16-point compass roses shown at right as a guide, create your own design. You may want to use various colors to enhance your compass rose.

11. Place your bowl of water, with the needle floating on a piece of paper, at the center of your compass rose. You now have a working magnetic compass.

The earth contains a core that is naturally magnetized. Because the earth is one big, albeit weak, magnet, a compass needle seeks to line itself up with the earth's magnetic field. In doing so, the compass needle always points toward the North Pole.

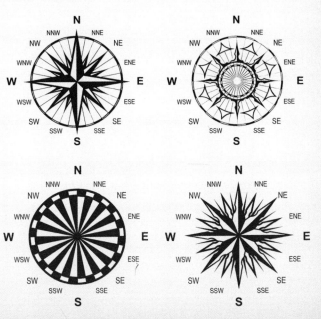

Abandoning plans to attack the Caribs, Columbus returned to Isabela on September 29, 1494. On arrival, he had to be carried from ship to shore. The Admiral of the Ocean Sea remained ill for five months.

While Columbus had been absent from Hispaniola, his appointed governing council was in control. They, in turn, had selected Alonso de Hojeda to be captain of a force of 400 men whose purpose was to relieve a garrison at Fort St. Thomas in the interior. On his way to the fort, Hojeda met three Spaniards. They told Hojeda that they had been robbed of some old clothes by a band of Indians. Hojeda, always ready to swing his sword at the slightest provocation, immediately ordered the ears of one Indian be cut off. Hojeda's overreaction was the first recorded instance of violence toward the friendly Arawak. There would be much more brutality to come.

Slave feeding caged birds.
Thinkstock 112706749
(collection: Dorling Kindersley RF)

Tensions Escalate

WHEN COLUMBUS disembarked at Isabela on September 29, a great surprise greeted him: his brother Bartholomew. Two years younger than the Admiral, Bartholomew arrived on Hispaniola on June 21, 1494. He had been, all his life, a supporter of everything Columbus sought to achieve. Bartholomew was a man of strong will and temperament who knew how to command, was decisive, and was remarkably free of arrogance, and yet displayed a great sense of authority. Thus, in many ways, he was the opposite of Columbus.

Their personality differences aside, Columbus appointed Bartholomew the **adelantado**,

Christopher Columbus firing a cannon, with Taino tribesmen standing nearby.
Thinkstock 125176212 (collection: Dorling Kindersley RF)

Indians, the soldiers rounded up 1,600 natives, including women and children, and brought them back to Isabela in chains.

In the fall of 1494, Antonio Torres returned to Isabela with four ships filled with supplies. It now became a question as to what to send back to Spain. The hope had been that the vessels could be filled with gold. While the shiny metal did exist on Hispaniola, there was not enough to truly impress. Columbus had a simple solution. Of the 1,600 captured Indians, 550 of the healthiest men and women were boarded to be taken to Spain as slaves. Approximately 600 others were parceled out to any Spaniards who wanted them. Of the 400 or so left, many women were mothers with infants. Many women felt they had no choice but to abandon their babies and flee into the mountains. They feared the Spanish, having no use for such "rejects," might simply kill them.

Torres's fleet left for the homeland on February 17, 1495. According to one eyewitness account:

When we reached the waters around Spain about 200 of those Indians died. I believe because of the unaccustomed air—colder than theirs. We cast them into the sea . . . when we reached Cadiz, in which place we disembarked all the slaves, half of them were sick. For your information they are not working people and they very much fear cold, nor have they long life.

an office equivalent to that of governor. Columbus remained viceroy.

As tensions escalated between the aggressive Spaniards and the increasingly daring Indians, Columbus decided to take bold action to crush an all-out rebellion before it happened. The Admiral sent a force into the interior where, after indiscriminately attacking and killing

Worse Than Slavery

On March 24, 1495, Columbus gathered 200 soldiers in full armor. They were equipped with **harquebuses** (muzzle-loaded rifles), lances, pikes, swords, and crossbows. Twenty vicious dogs were part of the company, as were 20 mounted cavalry. It was time, once and for all, Columbus felt, to subdue the island.

The army headed south, out of Isabela to the Vega Real (Royal Plain), 10 miles away. Here they expected to meet the enemy, those Indians the Spaniards had only recently promoted as gentle creatures. Though the friar Las Casas claims that 100,000 Arawak awaited the Europeans, the number was probably one-tenth that. From the moment the battle began, the Spaniards were in full control. They fired their harquebuses at point-blank range. And they loosed the dogs, which viciously ripped open bellies and tore off the limbs of their foes. In the end it was a complete slaughter. As one historian put it, "Of the valley that was Paradise they [the Spaniards] made a desert, and called it peace."

Caonabo, the most-feared cacique, remained at large. To apprehend him, Alonso Hojeda devised an ingenious trick. He invited Caonabo to accompany him back to Isabela where he would be given a prize church bell, an object the cacique valued dearly. On the way, Hojeda convinced Caonabo, who was placed upon a horse, to wear a pair of polished steel handcuffs and leg irons. Hojeda told Caonabo that this is how the king of Spain traveled. The cacique was thus captured and taken back to Isabela. Once there, he supposedly confessed to killing 20 of the 39 Spaniards left at La Navidad. Caonabo was shipped back to Spain, but died en route.

The island was now pacified. Any Spaniard could go anywhere without fear of being attacked. It was at this point that Columbus created his scandalous tribute system in which he hoped to extract gold (and spun cotton) from the Arawaks. Tribute led to the undoing of the Hispaniola Arawaks.

Each person above the age of 14 was required, every three months, to pay in gold dust a **hawk's bell** worth (about a thimbleful) of the rich metal. In areas where there was no gold, an Indian was required to furnish 25 pounds of spun cotton in the same period. Each Arawak who complied was given a stamped token to wear around his neck as proof of payment.

Even though the tribute was eventually lowered by half, the Indians could not find the required gold. As punishment for failing to comply, the Spaniards often cut a man's hands off. Others were simply killed. There was no way the Arawaks could meet their quotas. As Las Casas charged, "Even the cruelest of the Turks or Moors, or the Huns and Vandals

Panning for gold. Thinkstock 139891162 (collection: iStockphoto)

PAN FOR GOLD

CHRISTOPHER COLUMBUS and his fellow explorers knew there was gold in the West Indies, particularly on Hispaniola. In time, gold mines were opened in what is today Haiti and the Dominican Republic. But in the beginning, for the first decade after contact, those seeking gold sought an easier, if less rewarding, method of obtaining the precious metal. They panned for it in rivers and streams.

Gold found in running water is known as **placer** gold. It is the gold existing in deposits that have been eroded from solid rock. Nature, through erosion, grinds gold nuggets (chunks) out of rock and sends them downstream. The nuggets are mixed in with other rocks, sand, and debris. Wild stories aside, most nuggets are tiny little things, less than the size of a pea.

You can simulate the process of panning for gold. It is a fun and informative way to get the feel of what it must have been like for Columbus, his men, and enslaved Indians as they searched for the shiny metal.

Materials

+ a couple handfuls of small, rough rocks or gravel
+ Large tub
+ Wooden spoon
+ Water
+ Newspaper
+ Gold spray paint
+ Sand (bucketful)
+ Pie plate (metal or plastic, 8 to 10 inches in diameter)

1. Make gold nuggets. Choose a half dozen tiny rocks and wash them off. (Ideally, these rocks should be no larger than a pea, if not a grain of rice.) Dry the rocks and lay them out on newspaper. Spray paint each rock with gold paint. Set the rocks aside to dry fully.

2. Pour sand into a tub. Hide the nuggets in the sand along with a couple of handfuls of unpainted rocks. Mix everything up with the spoon—pretend you are stirring chocolate chips into cookie dough.

3. Add water to your tub. There should be enough water to cover the sand, plus 2 to 3 inches.

4. Using the pie plate, dig into the sand and water. Lift the plate out of the water and shake it a bit. Your pie plate should be filled with some of the sand mixture as well as some water. Stir the mixture with your free hand. From time to time, tilt your pie plate to allow some water to spill over the edge. Pick out the gold nuggets that you find. Repeat the panning procedure as often as you like.

who laid waste our kingdoms and lands and destroyed our lives, would have found such a demand impossibly onerous [demanding] and would have deemed it unreasonable and abhorrent [horrid]."

With the tribute system in place, any chance that the Arawaks would cooperate with the Spaniards in any other endeavor—supplying food, for example—evaporated. For ounces of gold dust, the colonists of Isabela gave up hope of receiving all other resources the land might offer—some of which were lifesaving.

In response to their trauma, thousands of the Arawaks reacted in the only way that gave them an out—a permanent reprieve. They committed suicide.

The Indians destroyed their stores of food so that neither they nor the Spaniards had access to them. Some poisoned themselves. Others jumped off cliffs. Many simply starved themselves to death. "Oppressed by the impossible requirement to deliver tributes of gold, the Indians were no longer able to tend their fields, or care for their sick, children, and elderly," wrote one historian. "They had given up and committed mass suicide.... It was an extraordinary act of despair and self-destruction, so overwhelming that the Spanish could not comprehend it."

How many Arawaks died by their own hand? Estimates range as high as 50,000.

MAKE A QUADRANT

WHILE A quadrant can be used to measure in degrees the altitude of a given object, its main use is to determine one's latitude on the earth's surface. As the illustration below shows, if one is standing on the equator, the North Star would be on the horizon. If the same person stood on the North Pole, the North Star would be almost directly overhead. As one moves north from the equator, the North Star appears to rise in the sky. The angle through which the North Star rises is equal to the change in the observer's latitude. If the North Star rises by 20 degrees, one has traveled 20 degrees of latitude.

As you use your quadrant to determine latitude (or altitude), you will find it is a challenge to keep the string from swinging. Imagine how difficult it was for Christopher Columbus to take a latitude reading while on the deck of a wave-tossed ship at sea.

NORTH STAR

N

EQUATOR

Materials

✛ Quadrant template
✛ Handle template
✛ Scissors
✛ Glue
✛ 1 piece card stock or cardboard (the back of a notepad works nicely)
✛ 1 foot of string
✛ Bead (weight)

CONSTRUCT THE QUADRANT

1. Photocopy the quadrant template and handle template from page 78.

2. Cut out the quadrant and handle.

3. Glue the quadrant template firmly to a piece of card stock. Trim the card stock away around the template shape.

4. Fold the handle along the dotted lines to form two tabs.

5. Glue the handle tabs to the back of the quadrant, so that the handle is parallel to the straight edge where indicated.

6. Punch a hole in the quadrant where indicated.

7. Tie one end of the piece of string through the hole.

8. Tie a bead (or suitable weight) to the other end of the string.

USE THE QUADRANT TO MEASURE THE ALTITUDE OF VARIOUS OBJECTS

1. Hold the quadrant to sight the top of a nearby building.

2. Let the string come to rest, pointing straight down.

3. Tilt the quadrant slightly so that the string touches the quadrant scale. With your finger and thumb, hold the string against the scale, bringing the scale end around where you can read it.

4. What you are reading is the height (altitude) of the building in degrees.

5. Try to sight other objects in the same manner.

USE THE QUADRANT TO MEASURE THE LATITUDE OF YOUR POSITION ON EARTH

1. If you live in the Northern Hemisphere, you will need to locate the North Star.

continued . . .

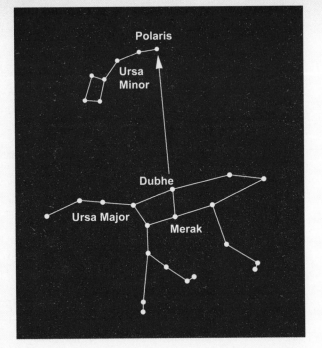

2. As the illustration above indicates, the North Star (Polaris) is at the end of the Big Dipper's handle.

3. Hold the quadrant to sight the North Star.

4. What you are reading is the latitude of your position on the earth's surface. For example, if you live in Los Angeles, the string should indicate an angle of 34 to 36 degrees.

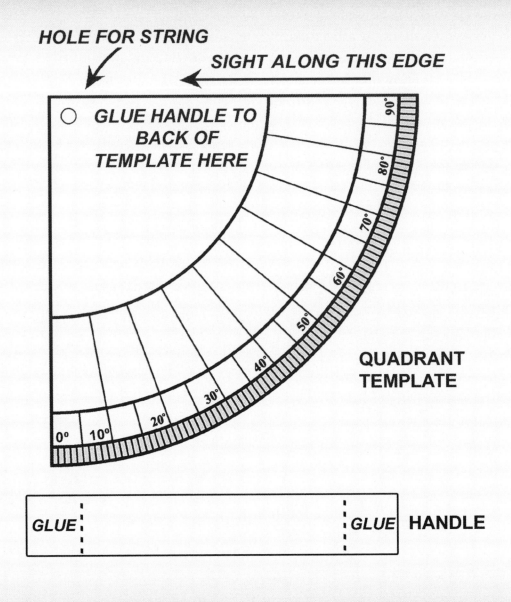

HOLE FOR STRING

SIGHT ALONG THIS EDGE

○ GLUE HANDLE TO BACK OF TEMPLATE HERE

QUADRANT TEMPLATE

90°
80°
70°
60°
50°
40°
30°
20°
10°
0°

GLUE | GLUE **HANDLE**

Mission Not Accomplished

IN OCTOBER 1495, Juan Aguado arrived at Isabela on a fact-finding mission for the sovereigns of Spain. The royal inspector, who had come out with Columbus on the second voyage and returned with the Antonio de Torres fleet, immediately assumed an authoritative manner. Though Aguado was expected to conduct an impartial investigation as to the cause of all the turmoil on Hispaniola, he sought testimony implicating the viceroy. Since about everyone in the colony was fed up and eager to go home, complaints poured in.

The situation on Hispaniola was indeed desperate. If a colonist was neither ill nor disaffected, he was inland, plundering at will. Most of the Spaniards still on Hispaniola in 1495, some 630, were of the *canalla* (low) class, not hidalgos who had, for the most part, already returned to Spain. Some of the *canalla* had clipped noses and ears, a sure sign of criminal background. As it was said of them, "It is hardly surprising that they spread with them the worst traits of conquistadorian cruelty and greed."

For Columbus, the time had come to return to Spain. The Admiral of the Ocean Sea needed to report to the king and queen and defend himself. Making his case would not be easy. Looting took place everywhere on

✠ The Treaty of Tordesillas

While Columbus was on his second voyage to the Indies, a treaty was concluded between Portugal and Spain that literally divided the world in half. Known as the Treaty of Tordesillas, it established a line of demarcation from the North Pole to the South Pole, 370 leagues (1,184 nautical miles) west of the Cape Verde Islands. Any new lands discovered west of the line would belong to Spain. Any new discoveries east of the line of demarcation went to Portugal. Signed in the town of Tordesillas, Spain, on June 7, 1494, the treaty was supposed to keep Portugal and Spain out of each other's territory, while allowing each country to discover what they may on its side of the line.

Since the line of demarcation was somewhere out there in the vast, mostly unexplored Atlantic, no one knew for sure where it was. While latitude, the distances north and south from the equator, could be determined with reasonable accuracy, longitude was another matter. It was not until the 18th century, with the invention of accurate timepieces, that sailors knew with certainty where they were to the east or west. Still, the Treaty of Tordesillas did draw a line, and for the most part, Portugal and Spain stayed away from each other while out exploring.

In signing the treaty, Portugal had hoped to keep exploration along the African coast their preserve. If they could do that and keep the Spanish from interfering, they could discover and monopolize a sea route to Asia. At the time, the Portuguese cared little for what Columbus was doing out there in the Antilles. They were not at all sure it would amount to much. As far as Portugal was concerned, they had received the better part of the bargain.

And, indeed, they may have. The line of demarcation, placed as it was 370 leagues west of the Cape Verde Islands, cut through the eastern part of South America—though at the time no European knew the continent even existed. That was enough to give Portugal what turned out to be the vast land of Brazil. With the Treaty of Tordesillas, Portugal established a presence in the New World—the world Columbus, though he would not acknowledge it as such, was busy discovering and exploring.

the island. Sickness, mainly from debilitating **dysentery**, was rampant. There was gold on Hispaniola, but not yet in the quantities that would cause the sovereigns to rejoice. And not a single Indian had yet been converted to the Catholic faith. For anyone willing to look with open eyes, failure was all about. It mattered little that it is doubtful any leader could have done better, given the kind of gold-hungry colonists who traveled with Columbus to the New World.

On March 10, 1496, Columbus, with two tiny ships, one of them the *Niña*, sailed for Spain. Both vessels were busting at the seams, not with gold and other treasure, but with people. There were 225 passengers aboard the two ships, including 30 Indians. The *Niña* normally carried two dozen men. Now it was weighed down with *five times* that many. "Where could they have been put?" one historian has asked. "What foul conditions must they have had to endure? What foul conditions must they have been escaping?"

It was a rough journey. For reasons that have never been satisfactorily explained, Columbus, the supreme navigator, decided to pursue a southerly route home. The Admiral had taken the northern route with great success on his first return voyage to Spain. On the southern path he would be bucking winds and currents almost all the way.

Six weeks out of the Indies, in early June, famine spread among the crew and passengers. Some suggested that the Indians should be killed and eaten. Others, supposedly more humane, advocated simply throwing them overboard to preserve the food sup-

Christopher Columbus writing by candlelight in a journal.

Thinkstock 84289920

(collection: Dorling Kindersley RF)

plies. Columbus, to his credit, said no to both schemes.

As the tiny fleet sailed closer to the European continent, the crews began to question their captain's competence, if not sanity. No land was in sight, and many felt he was way off course. But the choice of the southern route aside, if Columbus was anything, he was a superb navigator. On June 8, 1496, after nearly three months at sea, Columbus sighted the Portuguese coast. He had been aiming for Cape St. Vincent, just 35 miles to the south.

NORTH AMERICA

Atlantic Ocean

30N

Gulf of Mexico

BAHAMAS

25N

Straits of Florida

Tropic of Cancer

TO SPAIN

CUBA

20N

95W   90W   85W   80W   75W   70W   65W   60W

JAMAICA

15N

HISPANIOLA

Caribbean Sea

CENTRAL AMERICA

Pacific Ocean

MARGARITA   TRINIDAD

10N

FROM SPAIN

5N

COLUMBUS'S THIRD VOYAGE

SOUTH AMERICA

~ 6 ~

Earthly Paradise

U PON HIS ARRIVAL AT Cadiz on June 11, 1496, Christopher Columbus, now 45 years old, donned the coarse brown **habit** (clothing) of
a Franciscan friar. For the Admiral of the Ocean Sea, wearing the plain,
uncomfortable robe was a form of penitence. God, he was sure, was displeased
with him, with his lack of humility. Perhaps his misfortunes were due to his
outsized ego and pride. It was time to turn from sin.

Complaints about Columbus's governance of Hispaniola had preceded
his return to Spain. Rumors flew of near starvation conditions at the colony.
Little treasure of any kind had been found. Colonists were being ruled by a
tyrannical governor. Cruelty and lack of wealth was everyone's lot. The second
voyage, the expedition to establish a permanent foothold in the Indies, was
a failure, Columbus's critics insisted.

Columbus needed to defend himself. To that end, he left on the long, trying journey to Burgos, 500 miles from Cadiz, to meet his sovereigns. Upon hearing of his safe return, the king and queen had sent Columbus a gracious letter, dated July 12, 1496. The letter's tone gave the Admiral encouragement. Perhaps his detractors at court, of which there were many, had not succeeded in souring the mariner's reputation after all.

In the presence of Queen Isabella and King Ferdinand, Columbus was quick to assure the monarchs there was gold to be had on Hispaniola. He told the king and queen about discovering Jamaica, and about his long journey up the coast of Cuba. The latter, he insisted, backed by signed oaths, was probably the Malay Peninsula of southeast Asia. And, most important, Columbus tantalizingly told his sovereigns, Indians had assured him of a terra firma to the south of all the islands he had discovered. In other words, a continent. To confirm such a land's existence, a third voyage was necessary, the Admiral stressed.

No doubt to Columbus's pleasant surprise, the sovereigns were quite receptive to another voyage. In fact, they later issued an apology to the Admiral for having earlier sought to undermine his agreed-upon privileges:

> It never was our intention in any way to affect the rights of the said Don Christopher Columbus, nor to allow the conventions, privileges and favors which we have granted him to be encroached upon or violated; but on the contrary, in consequences of the services which he has rendered us, we intend to confer still further favors on him.

The Caribbean islands and the eastern coast of the Americas.

It was nearly two long years, however, before Columbus could embark on a third voyage. Among other events, the sovereigns were preoccupied with the royal wedding of their son and heir, Infante Don Juan, to the Archduchess Margarita of Austria. Twenty thousand guests attended the wedding. They were brought to Flanders and back to Burgos by 130 ships. The extravagant coupling nearly drained the royal treasury.

On May 30, 1498, when the third voyage was ready to begin, it had a different makeup than that of the second voyage. Upon the queen's orders, Columbus sought to recruit colonizers, not adventurers. To that end there were, among others, 20 mechanics, 40 servants, 30 sailors, 30 grommets (ship's boys), 20 miners, 10 gardeners, and 50 farmers. There were also 30 women on board.

Since stories of easy money were now scoffed at along the docks of Cadiz, it was necessary to open the jails and accept convicts willing to go on the third voyage. In exchange for a full pardon, those who had not committed first–degree murder, heresy, treason, arson, or counterfeiting were free to make the trip. Just how many chose to do so was not recorded. Yet Columbus never issued a complaint. It seems that on this voyage the Admiral had less trouble with his men than on his previous two journeys to the Caribbean.

A fortress on the coast of Cadiz, Spain. Thinkstock 93278994 (collection: iStockphoto)

South of the Antilles

SOON AFTER Christopher Columbus left Spain on the third voyage, he split his fleet of six ships. Three headed for Hispaniola, to supply the destitute colony at Santo Domingo. The remaining three ships, the discovery fleet, with the Admiral in command, took a southern route to the Indies. Its purpose was to discover lands lying south of the Antilles. According to the Greek philosopher Aristotle, it is near the equator, where it is hot, that gold, precious

MAKE HARDTACK

HARDTACK IS a hard, flat, unsalted cracker that resists spoiling, in some cases for up to 50 years. It was used by sailors in Columbus's day as a backup for food that would spoil or be consumed. Few sailors looked forward to eating hardtack, but doing so was better than starving. Know as "edible rocks," "hard bread," "tack," or "ironplate biscuits," hardtack was not designed to satisfy anyone's culinary taste. It was eaten grudgingly, when there was nothing else left.

Adult supervision required

Materials

✤ Bowl
✤ 1 cup water
✤ 1 teaspoon salt
✤ 2 cups flour
✤ Cutting board
✤ Rolling pin
✤ Knife or pizza cutter
✤ Wooden spoon
✤ Baking sheet

1. Preheat oven to 375° F.

2. Place the water and salt in the bowl, then slowly add flour while stirring constantly. Once the mixture has become too thick to stir, stop adding flour.

3. Scoop the mixture onto a lightly floured cutting board and knead (work with the hands) the dough. Then, using a rolling pin, roll the dough out until it is from ¼ to ½ inch thick.

4. Cut the dough into 3-by-3-inch squares with a knife or pizza cutter.

5. Using the handle end of a wooden spoon, poke 16 holes in each cracker, all the way through. You should have four rows of four holes each, for a matrix of 16 holes. The holes let steam escape.

6. Lay the crackers out on a lightly floured baking sheet.

7. Place in oven and bake for 30 minutes.

8. Remove from oven, flip crackers over, and bake for another 30 minutes.

9. Take the crackers out when they are a light golden brown.

10. Let the crackers cool for 30 minutes.

11. The next day, give your hardtack a second baking at a lower temperature, about 225° F for 30 to 45 minutes. A second baking finishes out the drying process.

If you wear braces or have fragile teeth, you may not want to bite into your crackers. Hardtack has no flavor. It has to take on the flavor of what it is soaked in (such as coffee, bacon grease, or butter). When properly made, hardtack can last for years. Since the purpose of this activity is to gain experience in making hardtack, not to satisfy your hunger, it may be best to discard what has been baked.

stones, and spices are found. Columbus understood that unless he discovered something new and profitable on this third voyage, the monarchs might pull the plug on his Enterprise of the Indies once and for all.

Although Columbus was thrilled to be out on the ocean again, where he was the most at home, throughout the third voyage the Admiral remained ill, at times seriously so. His son Ferdinand later reported that between Spain and the Cape Verde Islands, "The Admiral was suddenly seized by grievous pains of **gout** in the leg, and four days after, by a terrible fever." It soon became clear that Columbus's health problems were not just physical. He suffered from mental strains as well.

On July 13, 1498, the fleet entered the belt of calms, otherwise known as the **doldrums**. In such waters the winds die to almost nothing. Located just five degrees above the equator, it is also a place of extreme heat. As Las Casas wrote sometime later, no doubt with exaggeration:

So suddenly and unexpectedly did the wind drop and the extreme and unwonted heat strike them that no one would go below decks to see to the casks of wine and water, which burst and snapped their hoops. The wheat burnt like fire; the salt pork and other meat scorched and went bad. This heat lasted for eight days.

For the next two weeks, Columbus sailed west. Then, writing in his journal, the Admiral declared:

His Divine Majesty ever showeth mercy towards me, fortuitously [luckily] and by chance a seaman from Huelva, my servant named Alonso Pérez, climbed the crow's nest and saw land to the west, distance 15 leagues and it appeared to be in the shape of three rocks or mountains.

Christopher Columbus and a group of Spanish travelers greeting two tribal Indians.
Thinkstock 91284882
(collection: Dorling Kindersley RF)

Columbus had, on July 31, discovered Trinidad. Although he did not know it, he was in South American waters.

For 15 days Columbus explored the Gulf of Paria, between Trinidad and the South American mainland, near what is today Venezuela. It was here, where the mighty Orinoco River pours into the delta, that on August 4 the Admiral and his men experienced a frightening natural phenomenon. Probably caused by an underwater volcanic eruption, it nearly scared the crew to death:

> There came a current from the south as strong as a mighty flood, with such great noise and din that it terrified all hands, so that they despaired of escaping, and the ocean water which confronted it coming from the opposite direction, caused the sea to rise, making a great and lofty tidal wave which tossed the ship on top of the bore, a thing which none had ever heard or seen; and it tripped the anchors of the other vessel and forced her farther out to sea; and he made sail to get out of the said bore. It pleased God that they were not damaged.

Soon after this event, as Columbus sailed toward the west and saw that the Gulf of Paria had no outlet to the sea, he declared, "I have

The Garden of Eden. Thinkstock 136550127 (collection: iStockphoto)

before me a mighty continent which was hitherto unknown." Columbus then wrote to his sovereigns, "Your highnesses have an Other World (*Otro Mundo*) here by which our holy faith can be so greatly advanced and from which great wealth can be drawn."

Yet, four days later, on August 17, Columbus changed his mind. This Other World was not, he now judged, a new continent, but the oldest one of all. The Admiral believed he was on the outskirts of the earthly paradise. In a flight of fantasy, Columbus said he had found the Garden of Eden.

Furthermore, Columbus claimed that the ground he was now on was not spherical, but pear shaped. The Admiral concluded that at this latitude the Earth was not round. Indeed, here, on the northern coast of South America, Columbus was convinced the land was of a higher altitude than anywhere else on the planet. It was closer to heaven. Clearly, Columbus, probably due to utter exhaustion (he claimed to have gone 33 days without sleep—another exaggeration), was having a mental collapse.

An Admiral's Humiliation

ON AUGUST 16, 1498, Columbus, desperate to get to Hispaniola with what supplies he had, left the northern coast of South America and made a beeline for Santo Domingo. It took him three days of sailing to reach Hispaniola, and when he did, it was not at Santo Domingo, but 100 miles to the west. Still, it was an amazing feat of navigation, sailing from one uncharted island to another—something for which the Admiral of the Ocean Sea had now become justifiably respected.

Upon arrival off the coast of Hispaniola, Columbus gave orders to proceed north and west toward Santo Domingo. Within hours, his crew spied a small caravel approaching them and soon realized it was captained by Columbus's brother Bartholomew. Bartholomew had been appointed the *adelantado* (governor of a recently conquered province) at Santo Domingo by the Admiral two and a half years earlier. The two brothers embraced. It was a joyous occasion.

When Columbus finally arrived at Santo Domingo on August 31, he was utterly worn out. The Admiral was suffering from crippling **arthritis**. And he was almost, though only temporarily, blind. Columbus was desperate for some peace and quiet, some rest and relaxation. Instead, the Admiral found Hispaniola in a state of total rebellion.

In Columbus's absence, many colonists had died, some from outright starvation. Over 160 were said to have contracted a disease from the

MAKE A SUNDIAL

For thousands of years people had used sundials to tell the time of day. There is little doubt that Columbus and other contemporary explorers used them as well.

Over the course of the day, the sun appears to move across the sky. Of course, it isn't the sun that is moving; it is the earth as it rotates. But it is easier to regard the sun as being in motion.

For every 15 degrees that the sun appears to move, one hour in a 24-hour period transpires. All sundials have what is known as a **gnomon** (pronounced "no-men"). Its purpose is to cast a shadow on the face of the sundial. In this activity, you will use a pencil as a gnomon.

Each sundial must be made specifically for a particular region. This is because the sun shines differently around the globe. You can determine the latitude of where you live by searching on the Internet. Many websites have a form where you enter the name of your city and the site will tell you the latitude.

Materials

+ Sundial template
+ Scissors
+ Clear tape
+ A sharpened pencil
+ 1 piece card stock or cardboard (the back of a notepad works nicely)
+ Compass or map

1. Photocopy the sundial template shown on the opposite page 91.

2. Cut in from the edge of the template along the dotted lines (Line 1 and Line 3). BE SURE TO STOP AT THE SOLID LINE (Line 2).

3. Fold along the solid horizontal line (Line 2) with the line outside. Crease, then open flat again.

4. Fold along the solid vertical lines (Lines 5) with the lines outside. Crease, then open flat again.

5. Select the latitude line closest to your latitude. Fold along the latitude lines (Lines 4), and then tuck the fold to the inside. Tape in place.

6. Tape the paper sides to the base sheet.

7. Insert a sharp pencil point through the small circle. Twist the pencil as you make the hole.

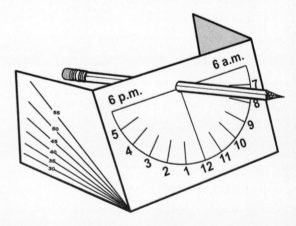

8. Remove the pencil and insert it in the hole with the eraser inside of the template as pictured above.

9. Tape the template to a flat piece of card stock. (If the pencil does not remain stable, tape the eraser end to the card to hold it in place.)

continued . . .

Sundial.

Thinkstock 93611727 (collection: iStockphoto)

10. Place the sundial outside in the sun. Use a map or compass to determine due north. Turn the sundial so that the pencil points due north.

11. If you cannot find due north, use a clock to determine the time. Then move the sundial until its time reading agrees with your clock. (If you are on daylight saving time, subtract one hour from the clock time.)

Check your sundial time against clock time for a few days. How do the times compare?

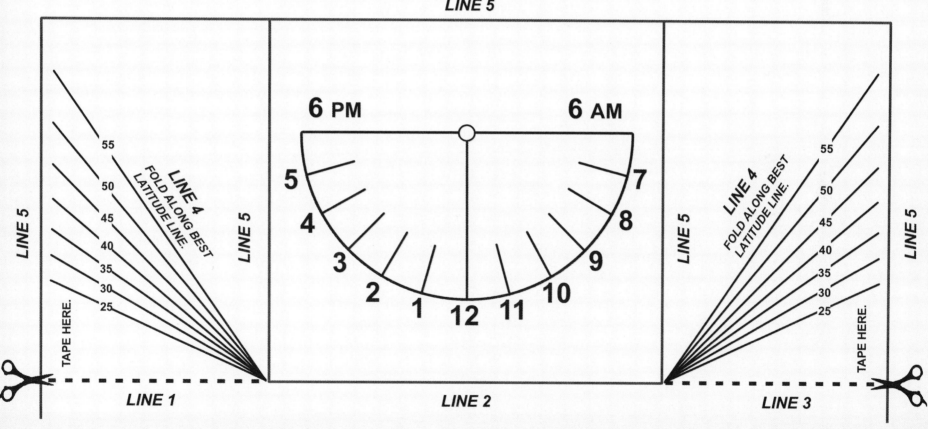

✠ "America's Birth Certificate"

In May 2003, the Library of Congress purchased the only surviving copy of one of the most remarkable maps ever produced. Known as the Martin Waldseemüller Map, and printed in 1507, the Library of Congress paid $10 million for the document, the most ever for a map by any institution, anywhere. Considering that the Waldseemüller Map has been christened, "America's Birth Certificate," the purchase was probably justified.

The map itself consists of 12 separate sheets, each 18 by 24 inches. When assembled, the map is huge—4 feet by 8 feet altogether.

The Waldseemüller Map is the first image of the world's continents as we know them today. It is the first document that shows a full, separate Western Hemisphere. It is the first map to depict the Pacific Ocean as a separate body of water. And, it is the first archive on which the name "America" appears.

The Waldseemüller Map is revealing in many ways. Most significantly, it is the first such map with the word "America" printed on it, on the southern continent. The name "America" probably comes from the feminized Latin version of Amerigo Vespucci's first name.

Vespucci, an Italian explorer and navigator, spent time along the northern coast of South America. In one of his many letters, it is claimed that Vespucci actually visited what is today Venezuela and the northern part of Brazil, in 1497. That would place the explorer on terra firma a year before Columbus's third voyage. Most scholars believe the letter is a fake. Vespucci, they argue, did not travel to the "Other World" until after Columbus.

Nonetheless, Vespucci is credited with being the first to recognize that Columbus and other explorers like him discovered a new continent unknown to Europe. For doing so, he was honored with the use of his name for the newly discovered lands.

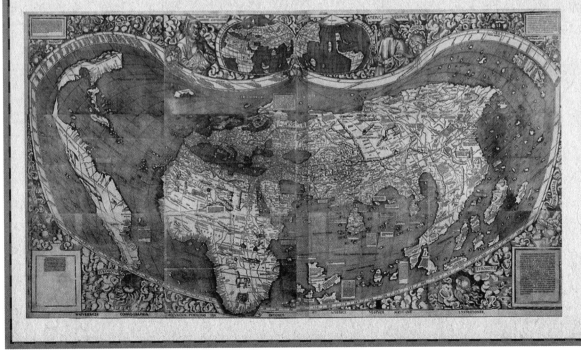

The Martin Waldseemüller Map of 1507 ("America's Birth Certificate").
ZephyrusBooks (OldBookArt.com) (Zazzle)

Arawaks, later identified as **syphilis**. In addition, colonists complained of too much work and not enough monetary reward. Gold was still hard to find. Food from Spain was not forthcoming in sufficient quantities. And, perhaps most important, many colonists had developed a deep hatred for the stern rule of the *adelantado*, Bartholomew Columbus—a foreigner.

To be successful, every rebellion needs a leader. The rebels found such a champion in Francisco Roldán, a man Columbus had earlier selected as the **alcalde mayor** (chief justice). As with most commanders, Roldán promised the world to those who joined his cause. To the Arawaks, there would be no more tribute demanded. For the Spaniards, they would be able to take up a life of leisure, with the Arawaks digging gold for them. Those colonists who wanted it would be given free passage home.

It was Roldán's purpose to overthrow the *adelantado*. Battles raged between Roldán's men and the *adelantado*'s supporters. The Arawaks chose sides based on which group of Spaniards promised to abuse them the least. There were times when it seemed a truce could be signed, ending the rebellion. But then fighting would begin anew.

In the end, it was up to Columbus to come to some accommodation with Roldán. Bar-

tholomew warned his brother Christopher that the only way to deal with Roldán was with tough and determined military force. Yet Columbus felt he had no such army at his command. Furthermore, the Admiral was aware that many men simply yearned to go home. Despite his poor health, Columbus decided to open negotiations with Roldán. In doing so he knew he was bargaining from a position of weakness.

In the end, Columbus wound up giving Roldán far more than he received in return.

ABOVE: *Gold nuggets.* Thinkstock 14679347 (collection: iStockphoto)

Marine iguana found throughout the West Indies and Central America. Thinkstock 123823589 (collection: iStockphoto)

Among the many concessions he requested, Roldán demanded and received full restoration to the office of alcalde mayor. There would be an official proclamation declaring that all charges against him had no basis in fact. Roldán's men who wished to remain on Hispaniola would be given free land grants.

The agreement between the two adversaries, signed on November 21, 1498, was a humiliating defeat for Christopher Columbus. Exhausted and in bad health, the Admiral wanted to go home. He eventually returned to Spain, but not until dishonor far worse would be heaped upon him.

Clamped in Irons

THE CONCESSION that Roldán won from Columbus, whereby the men who chose to remain in the Indies were given grants of land, proved to be the beginning of a New World feudal system. Known as **repartimiento** (distribution), to be followed by the **encomienda** (trust), the scheme that came to be was just short of outright slavery. The large acreage of farmland granted to a Spanish settler included ownership of the Indians living on it. The Indians provided tribute and labor. The Arawak agreed to this new economic arrangement in hopes of ridding themselves of the gold and cotton payment structure that was killing them off. The *encomienda* became a Spanish institution that lasted for centuries throughout Latin America.

It was at this time, in early September 1499, that four ships commanded by Alonso de Hojeda, an adventurer if there ever was one, arrived off the coast of Hispaniola. Earlier, while in Spain, Hojeda had obtained the charts sent back from the Gulf of Paria by Columbus. Hojeda, after some coaxing, obtained a license to sail to the region that Columbus had first discovered but was unable to explore in depth.

Hojeda, along with Amerigo Vespucci (whose first name would be given to the new continent), discovered valuable pearl fisheries in the region. While surveying the Gulf of Maracaibo, Hojeda renamed it Venezuela (Little Venice) because the native dwellings were on piles, reminding him of the Italian city. From northern South America, Hojeda headed for Hispaniola. Upon arrival he began to cut logwood, a tree native to the region.

By rights, Hojeda should not have been in the Indies at all. According to the agreement between Columbus and the sovereigns, only the Admiral could authorize such undertakings. Clearly, by allowing Hojeda an expedition to sail, the king and queen of Spain were displaying a lack of confidence in Columbus.

Pearl inside an oyster shell.
Thinkstock 106576182 (collection: iStockphoto)

Grow Shipboard Mold

When **Columbus** sailed to the West Indies, he did so in ships carrying European foods. The Admiral hoped the rations would stay edible for months. Yet, if not adequately preserved, usually by salting, such provisions would grow mold and become useless.

Salt preserves food in two ways. First, it removes the water from cells, thus drying them out. Second, salt can draw water out of some organisms that cause spoilage, killing them. In this activity, you will grow mold in a carefully controlled setting.

Adult supervision required

Materials

✛ 2 slices of tomato
✛ 2 slices of cheese
✛ 2 slices of bread
✛ Paper
✛ Pencil
✛ 3 tablespoons salt
✛ 6 large, clear resealable bags
✛ 6 clear, resealable plastic containers with lids

1. Write down your observations about each food slice: its size, shape, color, and texture.

2. Sprinkle at least one tablespoon of salt on one slice of each type of food—tomato, cheese, and bread. Leave the other three slices unsalted.

3. Place each food slice in separate container.

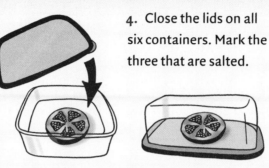

4. Close the lids on all six containers. Mark the three that are salted.

5. Place each resealable container in a resealable bag.

6. Place the six bags on a shelf or in a cabinet. Make sure the containers can't be reached by pets or little children.

7. Every day, for 10 days, check each slice. Write down your observations about them. Determine which food starts growing mold first. Is there a difference between mold growth on a salted food and an unsalted one?

8. After 10 days, ask an adult to dispose of or clean the Tupperware containers. Mold spores

are not good to smell or breathe.

Molds are a type of fungus. They grow from tiny spores that float in the air. Different molds tend to grow on different foods. They get energy and grow by breaking down plant or animal tissues.

While today refrigerators and preservatives keep moist foods from getting moldy, in Columbus's day salt was the most effective way to do so.

The Admiral's influence with the monarchs was waning.

As a reflection of this lack of trust, in the late spring of 1499, the sovereigns chose Francisco de Bobadilla, a servant of the crown and a knight, to sail to the Indies. Bobadilla was charged with investigating the deplorable conditions on Hispaniola. He was given the title of governor and chief magistrate by King Ferdinand and Queen Isabella. Bobadilla had the power to take over governance of Hispaniola. He carried with him a letter from the monarchs, addressed to Columbus, which read:

Don Cristóbal Colón [Christopher Columbus], Our Admiral of the Ocean. We have sent the Comendador Francisco de Bobadilla, the bearer of this letter, to say certain things to you on Our behalf. We desire you to place your full trust in him and pay him all respect, and to act accordingly.

Bobadilla's ship was delayed a year in sailing. But upon arrival in Santo Domingo, on August 23, 1500, the commander was greeted with a shocking sight. The corpses of seven rebels were hanging from the gallows near the shore.

The commander took immediate action. He halted the scheduled execution of five more rebels. And then, after taking testimony from disgruntled settlers, Bobadilla undertook the most outrageous act in the annals of the Christopher Columbus saga. The commander had the Admiral of the Ocean Sea, along with Bartholomew and Diego (Columbus's youngest brother, who had arrived earlier to help govern the colony) placed in irons and thrown in jail. They were to be sent back to Spain, shackled during the entire trip, to be tried and, if found guilty, sentenced.

Bobadilla had overreacted. In judging Columbus's governance of Hispaniola, it is doubtful anyone could have done much better, least of all a foreigner. It is true that Columbus had been a weak leader when he should have been stronger. And there were times when the justice he dispensed was ruthless and wrong. But in a letter written on his return voyage, or soon after landing in Spain, the Admiral of the Ocean Sea made a case for the impossibility of his task:

In Spain, they judge me as if I had been a governor of Sicily, or in some well-ordered city or town, where laws can be kept to the letter, without risking total disaster. I feel that this is completely unjust. I should be judged as a captain who has gone from Spain to the Indies, to conquer a numerous and warlike nation, whose customs and beliefs are entirely different from ours, who live in the highlands and among the mountains, with no abiding habitations, where, by the Grace of God, I have brought a new world into the dominions of Our Sovereigns the King and Queen of Spain, whereby Spain, which was once held to be poor, is now the wealthiest of countries.

Indeed, the Indies that Columbus discovered were not yet, as some would try to make them, the homeland of Spain.

ing them, as did the colonists when the three sailed from Santo Domingo, they became angry at their treatment. When the sovereigns heard the news, they ordered the brothers set free. They also sent them 2,000 **ducats**, so that when the three arrived at court, they would do so in a dignified manner.

On December 17, 1500, Christopher Columbus and his two brothers presented themselves at the Spanish court in Alhambra.

La Mota Castle in Valladolid, Spain.
Thinkstock 99486110 (collection: Hemera)

Viceroyalty Denied

AT THE beginning of October 1500, Columbus boarded the caravel *La Gorda* to be taken to Spain to be tried along with his two brothers. When the ship left the harbor, the captain offered to free Columbus from his chains. The Admiral refused. With a **martyr's** (a person who voluntarily suffers) touch, typical of the mariner, Columbus later declared that, "He had been placed in chains in the sovereigns' name and would wear them until the sovereigns ordered them removed." Columbus kept the shackles by him until his death, and he ordered that they be buried with his body.

La Gorda arrived at Cadiz on November 20, having completed the Atlantic crossing in record time. When the people saw the Admiral and his brothers in chains, instead of taunt-

✠ Columbus's Signature

```
        ·S·
      ·S· A ·S·
       X   M   Y
    :χρoƒERENS./
```

Christopher Columbus had an unusual way of signing his name—at least it is different when compared to the way we sign our names today. As Columbus's signature above shows, it consists of a pyramid of letters. Close to 50 of these signatures have been found, always with the letters arranged as such. In a few cases, the last line is read differently, with *virey*, the viceroy, stated.

Columbus attached great importance to his signature. He insisted that his heirs were to always "Sign with my signature which I now employ which is an X with an S over it and an M with a Roman A over it and over that an S and then a Greek Y with an S over it, preserving the relation of the lines and points."

Columbus never revealed just what it all meant. As a consequence, for the last 500 years, there has been endless speculation about the Admiral's signature.

By inverting or reading some of the letters, one can make almost anything of the monogram. Some scholars insist it proves that Columbus was a Jew. Others say it means he was a Freemason.

The historian Samuel Morison says that the third line is probably an invocation to Jesus Christ and Mary (Christe, Maria, Yseu). The first four letters, Morison notes, lend themselves to almost countless combinations, the simplest being, "Servant I am of the Most High Savior."

The final line, χρoƒERENS, is, according to Morison, simply a Greco-Latin form of Columbus's given name. It is a reminder that by baptism he was consecrated to the task of carrying the word of God overseas to **heathen** lands.

It seems when it comes to Christopher Columbus, the old saying, "What's in a name?" or signature, has many answers.

It was a highly emotional encounter. Columbus broke out into sobs as he kissed the hands of the king and queen. The flow of tears continued as the Admiral assured the monarchs that if he had committed errors, they were because of ignorance and inexperience, not evil intent.

The queen was deeply moved by Columbus's plea. The sovereigns, she said, had never intended that he be imprisoned. They would see to it that those responsible were punished (though Bobadilla, for one, never would be).

Columbus, his highnesses now declared, would be given restoration of all income, rights, and possessions taken from him by Bobadilla. However, the Admiral did not regain his own title of viceroy. He would no longer rule the Indies as the monarch's representative.

In truth, King Ferdinand, who had never liked Columbus, had come to the conclusion that while the Admiral was unsurpassed on the ocean, he could not be trusted to govern on land. The king had not anticipated that so much territory and wealth would become available. In the future, the sovereigns would take control of all that was to be had; it would not be left in the hands of a foreigner.

It is ironic that at this very time, during the mismanaged third voyage, Hispaniola began to produce what every Spaniard had been praying for—significant amounts of gold.

What Columbus had been talking about all these years was finally coming true. There was, indeed, gold in the hills of Hispaniola. Now, and for years to come, the island furnished from one to three tons of the precious metal every year. Columbus, however, shared little in the gold rush now underway on Hispaniola.

If the Admiral fell into a funk regarding the events now surrounding him, he must have become downright depressed on hearing of an earth-shaking voyage that occurred while he was in the Indies. In 1499, Vasco da Gama had returned to Portugal with remarkable news. He had accomplished what everyone, including Columbus, had been trying to do. Da Gama, sailing around Africa, had continued on, completing a sea route to Asia (India).

In order to distinguish what da Gama had discovered by sea, the East Indies, the islands in the Caribbean then became known as the West Indies. Even Columbus was prepared to call them such.

~ 7 ~

The High Voyage

IN 1500, THE DAWN of a new century, Christopher Columbus was deep into retirement age. Even though he was only 49, for the times he lived in, the man from Genoa was considered old. Furthermore, given the Admiral's lifestyle, it was a wonder he was still alive. In truth, he barely was.

Considering Columbus's catalog of illnesses, if anyone deserved some rest and relaxation, it was him. The last thing the aging mariner, half-blind, disabled with arthritis, and ill with **malaria** fever, should have been thinking of was another grueling voyage to the West Indies. Yet, that is what Columbus hoped for. Discovery and exploration were in the Admiral's bones. He would do it until he was simply no longer able. Columbus needed one more voyage, if only to redeem himself. But, given all that had happened, who would sponsor a fourth expedition?

On February 13, 1502, a new fleet did leave for the West Indies. It consisted of 30 ships and 2,500 persons, including 73 married men with their families. Columbus, however, was not on board.

The man in charge of this massive squadron was Nicolás de Ovando. He was being sent to Hispaniola to replace Bobadilla as governor. Ovando took with him 72 squires as his bodyguards, 10 of whom were horsemen. It was a new era in colonization. From now on, living and working on Hispaniola would be for those who wished to settle, not plunder.

✛ Book of Prophecies

The *Book of Prophecies* was written by Columbus in an attempt to interest his sovereigns in greater enterprises. All such undertakings would have biblical and religious foundations.

In one endeavor, Columbus proposed the amassing of an army of 50,000 foot soldiers and 5,000 cavalry. Their purpose would be to march on Jerusalem and drive out the infidels. In the process, the soldiers would recover the holy **sepulcher** (sacred tomb). How would this army be paid for? From the wealth Columbus assured the monarchs he would bring back from a fourth voyage.

In the *Book of Prophecies*, Columbus also sought to place himself in the grander scheme of things. He insisted that the discovery of America was part of God's plan. Columbus was the chosen one to lead that discovery and exploration. To finish the job, he would need a fourth expedition.

But Columbus wasn't cast aside just yet. While the sovereigns wanted a new administration on Hispaniola, one that would establish true settlements, they also realized that discovery and exploration were still essential. And the monarchs knew that while Columbus had shown himself to be a poor administrator, there was no better navigator and explorer. Thus they were prepared to sponsor a fourth voyage led by Columbus. There was one major condition, however: Columbus was to steer clear of Hispaniola altogether. Once he arrived in the West Indies, the Admiral was to head further west in hopes of finding a **strait** through which he could then sail on to Asia. In other words, the explorer was to stick to doing what he did best: discovering.

Columbus left Cadiz with four ships, *La Capitana*, *Santiago*, *La Gallego*, and the *Vizcaína*, on May 9, 1502. None would ever return to Spain.

Columbus's crew consisted of 139 sailors—40 percent of whom were mere "ship's boys," some only 12 or 13 years old. One 13-year-old was Ferdinand, Columbus's youngest son. With all the sailing his father had been doing, at the time of the fourth voyage Ferdinand barely knew his dad.

Ferdinand gave up the cushy life as royal page in the Spanish court, and he would need to prove himself as a seaman. It was not an easy life for any 13-year-old, let alone the son of the fleet's commander. Above all, Ferdinand had to demonstrate the ability to keep his mouth shut. Crew members might assume the young Ferdinand would be only too willing to spy for his father by passing along ship's gossip not intended for the Admiral's ears. For Ferdinand, this was not a pleasure cruise. Still, it could be a trip of a lifetime, one that could turn a boy into a man.

After a stop in the Canary Islands, the fleet's voyage to the West Indies took only 21 days, making it one of the fastest transatlantic passages Columbus ever undertook. The Admiral anchored off Martinique Island, in the Lesser Antilles, on June 15, 1502.

Against orders, Columbus now sailed straight for Hispaniola. The Admiral wished to find a replacement ship for the *Santiago*, which he felt was too slow. Crossing from Martinique to Santo Domingo proved a smooth passage. For the crew it was like sailing through paradise.

Hurricane Madness

TO BE a great navigator in the age of sail required many skills. Top among them was that of weathercaster. Though the barometer, an instrument used to measure air pressure, would not be invented for another century,

Columbus could, given his arthritic condition, literally feel a change in the weather in his bones. His joints now told him that the air pressure off Hispaniola was behaving suspiciously. That, along with the Admiral's years of sailing experience (observing cirrus clouds, oily seas, and abnormal tides) convinced him that a storm was brewing. Columbus could smell it coming. Today, we know such a storm as a hurricane.

Ovando, fearing a rival to his authority, refused to let Columbus anchor down to shelter his fleet in the Santo Domingo harbor. Even with that rebuke, the Admiral was quick to warn Ovando of the impending deluge. Ovando's fleet of 28 ships was preparing to leave on a homeward journey the very next day, June 30. There would be hundreds of people aboard, and Columbus begged Ovando to delay sailing for at least eight days, when the hurricane would then have passed. Ovando merely scoffed at the Admiral.

On the 30th, with Ovando remaining in Santo Domingo, his return fleet sailed out of the harbor, **tacking** east into the wind, heading for Spain. Columbus, too, sailed out, but turned west, seeking a natural port or protective cove. Should he not find one, the Admiral was sure everyone on board would perish.

Columbus's men were angry. Many believed their lives were being put in danger because of the hostility between Ovando and their Admiral. If it weren't for that hatred, they reasoned, the men would not have been denied a safe harbor.

After sailing 45 miles, Columbus came across a horseshoe-shaped indentation known as Ocoa Bay. Here his ships dropped their anchors.

The men scurried below deck. They shared the smelly space with stores and rats. Winds of more than 100 miles per hour slammed their ships. Rain fell in thick drops, sounding like hail as it hit the deck. Father and son huddled together in Columbus's small cabin.

In the middle of the night, the *La Gallego*, *Vizcaína*, and the *Santiago* were ripped from their anchorages and thrown out to sea. "The storm was terrible," Columbus wrote, "and on that night my fleet was broken up. Everyone lost hope and was quite certain that all the rest were drowned."

Bad as it was for Columbus and his crew—miraculously no ships or crew members were

(LEFT) *A hurricane system, as seen using satellite imagery.*
Thinkstock 140238249 (collection: iStocktrek Images)

(RIGHT) *Tornado over the water.*
Thinkstock 117553732 (collection: iStockphoto)

Early European explorers to the Caribbean found that while at times the weather was just fine, there were also times when storms the likes of which they had never known could rise up and drown them. Known as hurricanes, from the Carib Indian word *hurican*, meaning "evil wind," these storms can blow with swirling winds in excess of 150 miles per hour. Accompanied by incredible rates of rainfall, hurricanes can easily produce waves that will swamp a good-size ship when out at sea.

The formation of a hurricane occurs when centripetal (inward) and centrifugal (outward) forces are applied to a system with varying densities such as water and air, which exists with a hurricane over water. The result is a **vortex** (whirlpool), a vacuum that draws in its path anything that is not firmly anchored down. In this experiment, you will create a vortex in a bottle.

Materials

✚ 2 empty 2-liter bottles
✚ Scissors
✚ Cold water
✚ Food coloring (any color)
✚ 4-inch length of 13/16-inch outer diameter PVC pipe
✚ Glue
✚ Duct tape (or similar)
✚ Bits of paper to float in water

1. Remove the outer labels from your bottles. You may want to save the labels to cut up, making bits to float in the water.

2. Fill one bottle half full with water.

3. Squeeze a couple of drops of food coloring into the water.

4. Drop a handful of paper pieces into the bottle containing water.

5. Insert the 4-inch length of PVC pipe into the opening of the bottle containing water. Place the PVC pipe halfway in (about 2 inches).

6. Glue the PVC pipe to the bottle opening. Spread plenty of glue.

7. Immediately flip the second bottle upside down and place it on top of the PVC pipe that is sticking up. Press the second bottle down so that its neck

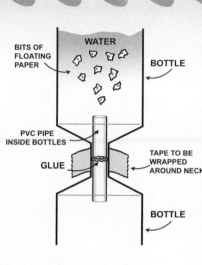

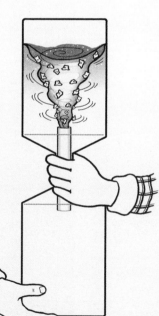

touches the lower bottle's neck. If necessary, spread the glue so that it makes a good covering for both bottles. Let the glue dry completely.

8. Cut the duct tape to size and apply liberally around the connection joint to complete the seal.

9. To create a vortex, flip the bottles over and rotate them in a rapid clockwise or counterclockwise direction. Periodically halt your rotation and observe the vortex being created. Repeat as often as you like.

Notice that as the water empties, the bits of paper move faster near the bottom of the vortex, illustrating centrifugal force. Furthermore, the vortex should be more visually pronounced because the water is colored.

lost—for the squadron of 28 ships that left for Spain, the hurricane was an all-out disaster.

The Spanish fleet was under the command of Antonio de Torres. Soon after leaving Santo Domingo, his ships began to separate. In no time they were widely strung out. As they turned northeast, the vessels headed directly into the path of the approaching hurricane.

The raging sea swallowed many ships outright. Those that attempted to make it back to shore were broken to pieces as they slammed against coastal rocks. In all, more than 500 sailors and passengers drowned.

Among the unfortunate was Bobadilla, the man who had placed Columbus in irons two years earlier.

Gone, too, was King Ferdinand's ransom of gold, including a nugget reported to have weighed 35 pounds.

Only 4 of the 28 Spanish ships survived. One that did was the *Aguja*. It contained Columbus's post-arrest settlement—240,000 in gold *maravedís*. When gathered back in Spain, it made Columbus a wealthy man.

Was it divine providence that saw Bobadilla drown, while the Admiral's gold was saved? Ferdinand, Columbus's 13-year-old son, was sure it was God's doing.

Searching for a Strait

WITH THE hurricane over and Columbus's four ships in need of repair, the Admiral and his crew took a much-deserved time-out. Some men went fishing. A group from the *Vizcaína* harpooned a ray the size of a small bed and delighted as it dragged them and their small boat through the water before it died. Others caught a manatee, also called a sea cow, which was then unknown in Europe. Big as a calf, the men chopped up the "fish" (though it is actually a mammal) and ate it. Some claimed the manatee tasted better than a cow.

(RIGHT) *Swimming manatee.*
Thinkstock 138186925 (collection: iStockphoto)

(LEFT) *Ray.* Thinkstock (photographer: Hemera Technologies) 87566730 (collection: photoObjects.net)

It was then July 14, 1502, and time to steer west. Columbus stopped briefly at Jamaica and then pushed further on to Cuba, a familiar landfall. But when the Admiral reached the western end of the big island, he knew any further sailing would take him into the unknown. Had Columbus now voyaged directly west, he might have encountered the Yucatán Peninsula and its advanced Mayan civilization. Instead, the Admiral journeyed southwest. After racing ahead for 360 miles in just three days, he reached the offshore island of Bonacca. Columbus was now only a few miles from Honduras, part of the Central American mainland.

It was at this time that a huge canoe as long as a galley ship—eight feet wide and cut from a single tree—approached the Spaniards. The craft was filled with 25 men and 15 women and children. The men in the canoe wore sleeveless shirts and carried hatchets made of copper. Columbus was convinced they represented a relatively advanced civilization from the mainland. The Spaniards captured the canoe and helped themselves to its cargo of colored shawls and wooden swords, among other objects. Columbus forcibly retained the canoe's skipper to use as an interpreter. Taking leave of Bonacca, the Admiral sailed on, arriving on the Honduran coast on July 30.

Columbus now proceeded almost due east. What happened during the next 38 days made the Admiral and his crew often wish they had never left Spain. They anchored off the coast every night, and every day they beat against contrary winds that forced them to tack (change directions by turning the **bow** into the wind) all the way. In those five-plus weeks, the fleet traveled only 200 miles. Torrential winds ripped their sails. What the crews gained by tacking they often lost to the currents rushing against them. Tropical storms drenched everything. The ship's hulls flooded, ruining most provisions. Working the pumps became a constant—24 hours a day, every day. Columbus later declared:

> My people were very weak and humbled in spirit, many of them promising to lead a religious life, and all making vows and promising to perform pilgrimages, while some of them would frequently go to their messmates to make confession. Other tempests have been experienced, but never so long a duration or so fearful as this.

Through it all, Columbus remained determined, though his poor health was sapping his strength. As a consequence, the Admiral had a small cabin (known as a doghouse) built atop the **poop deck** of his flagship. From there he could observe the goings-on even as he lay flat.

When the coast of Central America finally turned south, the storms subsided. By early

October, the fleet was coasting along what is today Panama. Local Indians told the Admiral that it was only nine days' journey across the **isthmus**. On the other side was an ocean every bit as large as the Atlantic. The Indians were, of course, talking about the Pacific. Columbus and his men, however, were not equipped to make an exhausting trek through the Panamanian jungle. They remained Atlantic bound.

Though the Spaniards could not cross the isthmus that would one day be spanned by the Panama Canal, they were heartened by all the gold they were finding in the region known as Veragua (Panama). For the next two weeks Columbus's fleet sailed down the coast, eagerly trading trinkets for the gleaming metal.

Soon enough, the weather again turned bad. It was time to make camp and, if possible, establish a permanent presence on the mainland. From such a base the Spaniards could extract all the gold available. The sovereigns, Columbus was sure, would be pleased.

The new settlement that Columbus ordered to be built was called Santa María de Belén. In the end, it never took hold.

Over the next many months, the crew of Columbus's ships interacted with the local people, all the while sailing back and forth along the scorching coast, collecting as much gold as possible.

At times there was peace and trading. Often the young boys on board would sneak off at night to rummage around on the shore.

There were other times, however, when outright war raged between Spaniards and natives. In one bizarre incident, a brave Christian, Diego Mendez, confronted a large group of hostile Indians by calmly sitting down in front of them, and taking out a comb, scissors, and mirror. He then started cutting his companion's hair. Dumbfounded, the Indians let the two escape.

Panamanian tropical forest.
Thinkstock 149406295 (collection: iStockphoto)

Columbus, suffering mightily from his usual ailments, at one point almost gave up the ship, literally and figuratively. The 51-year-old Admiral climbed atop its tallest mast and begged the heavens for help:

"Crying in a trembling voice, with tears in my eyes, to all your Highnesses' war captains, at every point of the compass to save me," he later wrote. "But there was no reply." Exhausted, the Admiral of the Ocean Sea retired to his cabin and sobbed himself to sleep.

It was time to leave. The explorers had not discovered a strait, but they had come across a new source of gold. That, reasoned Columbus, would have to be enough for the monarchs.

On May 1, 1503, Columbus, with two **shipworm**-infested ships, *La Capitana* and the *Santiago*, sailed away from the coast of Panama. Amazingly, throughout the entire nine-month ordeal just concluded, Christopher Columbus may never have set foot on Central American soil. So racked with pain, he probably remained shipboard the entire time.

Christopher Columbus and the Arawak Indians.
Thinkstock 104572393 (collection: Dorling Kindersley RF)

Striking for Jamaica

COLUMBUS NOW set a course for Hispaniola, although some crew members initially feared he would try a run all the way to Spain. *La Capitana* and the *Santiago* were slowly but surely sinking as shipworms bored into them. There was no way the two vessels would ever reach Europe. They would be lucky, jammed as they were with too many men, to make Hispaniola.

By May 10, the small fleet had crossed the Caribbean Sea, but in an uncommon failure of navigation, Columbus missed both Hispaniola and Jamaica. He was once again on the western coast of Cuba.

It was quickly decided that a run for Hispaniola would be suicide. The only sensible plan now was to try to strike for Jamaica. As Ferdinand later wrote:

We stood over toward Jamaica because the easterly winds and the strong westward-running currents would have never let us make Hispaniola—especially since the ships were so riddled by the shipworm that day and night we never ceased working three pumps in each of them.

By June 23, the water levels in both ships had reached nearly to their decks. Finally, two days later, the fleet made Jamaica. Ferdinand continued:

Having got in, since we were no longer able to keep the ships afloat, we ran them ashore as far as we could, grounding them close so they could not budge; and the ships being in this position the tide rode almost to their decks.

It was June 25, 1503. Columbus and 116 sailors were stranded on Jamaica with little prospect of rescue. Here they remained for a year and five days.

✠ Shipworms

The shipworm is not actually a worm but an unusual saltwater clam. No matter, it looks like a worm, one that can grow to over three feet in length. The clam feeds off wood immersed in seawater. Thus a wooden ship is a prime target. When the clam gorges on a wooden hull, it bores a hole in it. With more shipworms there are more holes. With enough holes, a ship will begin to look like Swiss cheese. When there are more holes than wood, the ship is in danger of sinking.

The process of boring is gradual at first but it cannot be stopped. The shipworm usually enters the hull of a ship in its larva stage. Then, as it grows longer and longer, it consumes more wood. If a ship is out to sea when this is happening, the crew's prospects are dire. The only thing the sailors can do is to keep pumping and bailing water in the hope of reaching land before the ship sinks.

Marooned

AT FIRST, the Arawak of Jamaica were peaceful and hospitable. They eagerly traded food for trinkets. But Columbus was apprehensive. Eventually the hawk's bells would run out. Why, then, the Admiral figured, would the Arawak continue to supply the Spaniards with provisions?

On July 7, Columbus selected two men, Diego Mendez and Bartolomeo Fieschi, to undertake an almost impossible task. They, along with a half dozen Arawak paddlers, were to take an Indian canoe across 100 miles of ocean to Hispaniola to seek help. The chances of success were not good.

After one false start on July 17, both Spaniards (each now in his own canoe), along with Indians to paddle, tried again.

The first day was easy going, though the heat was intolerable. At times, the Indians would leap into the ocean to cool off. During the night, the paddlers took turns; while half slept, the other half paddled. In spite of the periodic rests, by daybreak the Arawak were dangerously exhausted. Furthermore, it was discovered that the Indians, not thinking ahead, had drunk all their water. Though the captains had maintained a meager supply, if the canoes did not reach land soon, all would perish.

Finally, the men spotted the small island of Navassa. The parched sailors landed. The Indians eagerly drank the rainwater trapped in the hollows of rocks. The Spaniards cautioned the Arawaks against drinking too much water after being so dehydrated. They did not listen. As a result, some vomited water back up.

Prophet Jonah swimming away from the open mouth of a large whale.

Some, with the rainwater overwhelming their systems, died.

Drained, exhausted, and barely able to move, the next day the crews reached the western edge of Hispaniola. The Spaniards, after four days of hell, felt as if they had been delivered from the whale's belly, like the prophet Jonah. It is hard to know what the surviving Arawak were thinking.

Dugout canoe. Thinkstock 1402270783 (collection: iStockphoto)

Rescue at Last

As 1503 turned into 1504, six months had passed and no one on Jamaica had heard from Mendez or Fieschi. Most assumed they had drowned. The marooned men were growing despondent and bitter. On January 2, 1504, all-out anger displayed itself in mutiny. Half of the Spaniards, led by two brothers, Francisco and Diego de Porras, rebelled.

At one point, the mutineers piled into 10 dugout canoes, along with dozens of Indian paddlers, and headed out to sea. "The Porras brothers and their merry men started eastward along the coast 'as gaily as if they had been in some harbor of Castile,' robbing the Indians wherever they called, and telling them to collect their pay from the Admiral, or kill him if they could," wrote Samuel Eliot Morison.

But soon enough, the weather turned hostile, and the mutineers resorted to throwing everything overboard but their arms. Then, they tossed the Indians into the ocean. When some tried to cling to the sides of a canoe, the Spaniards chopped off their hands. The mutineers returned to Jamaica, where, before they finally surrendered to the Admiral, they broke into wandering groups, resuming their exploitation of the land and its native people.

As Columbus expected, the Arawak had finally grown tired of supplying food to the

Spaniards, who, according to Ferdinand, could consume 10 times what an Indian ate. In February, the Indians upped the price while lowering the food portions. If this continued, Columbus and his men would starve.

It was at this time that Columbus remembered 1504 was a leap year, with 29 days in February. Furthermore, on February 29, there would be an eclipse of the moon. Knowing these facts, Columbus came up with a clever plan.

Columbus gathered all the local Arawak chiefs on the evening of February 29. He told them that his Christian God was angry with them for holding back on food. To show his displeasure, God would punish the islanders by taking light away from the moon. When the moon, indeed, began to disappear as a result of the eclipse, the Indians panicked. They begged Columbus to intercede. The Admiral agreed, the moon began to shine again, and the Arawak reestablished hardy food deliveries.

Contrary to the marooned men's assumptions, Mendez and Fieschi had not drowned. But Governor Ovando was determined to delay the sailing of any rescue ship. When the citizens of Santo Domingo heard of the governor's neglect, they were outraged. In late June, Ovando allowed two vessels to leave for Jamaica. When they arrived, Columbus and his men were overjoyed.

✚ Book of Privileges

In the 16 months between the end of his third voyage and the beginning of his fourth, Christopher Columbus had much time on his hands. He used it to produce two books: the *Book of Privileges* and the *Book of Prophecies*. With both he hoped to make his case for continued support from the Spanish sovereigns.

The *Book of Privileges* was, essentially, a large notebook. In it, Columbus placed 44 documents that he hoped would reinforce his case for titles, awards, rights, and offices that he insisted were still owed him. Four copies of the *Book of Privileges* were made. One of them is now in the archives of the United States Library of Congress.

Unfortunately for Columbus, the monarchs of Spain, in particular King Ferdinand, paid little attention to the Admiral's efforts. The sovereigns honored Columbus, but they also replaced him. Most of the titles he was left with were of no real value.

The return trip from Jamaica to Hispaniola took three weeks, not the four days it had taken Mendez and Fieschi. The ship they sailed on, the *Caravelón*, was not in good shape. Its mainmast was broken, the sails rotten, and the bottom foul. The *Caravelón* leaked so badly, it was difficult to keep it afloat. Nonetheless, Columbus was back in Santo Domingo on August 13, 1504.

The phases of a lunar eclipse.
Thinkstock 1198865 (collection: iStockphoto)

SIMULATE A LUNAR ECLIPSE

BY KNOWING when a total lunar eclipse would occur, Columbus was able to frighten the Arawaks of Jamaica into believing they had angered the Admiral's God. In a lunar eclipse, the moon is eclipsed—that is, it is hidden or covered. The earth, being between the moon and the sun, blocks the sun's rays from illuminating the moon. As the moon, traveling in its orbit, enters the earth's shadow (called the "umbra shadow"), the eclipse begins. As the moon continues on its course, it emerges from the earth's shadow and the eclipse ends. You can simulate your own lunar eclipse.

Materials

✛ 2 sharpened pencils
✛ 3-inch Styrofoam ball
✛ Modeling clay
✛ Ruler
✛ Flashlight
✛ 2 to 4 books
✛ Drawing compass
✛ 3-inch square of white poster board
✛ Scissors

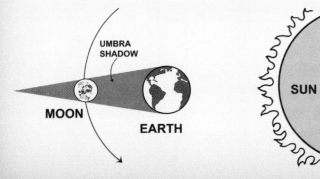

1. Insert about 1 inch of the sharpened end of a pencil into the Styrofoam ball.

2. As pictured, use clay to stand the pencil on a table about 12 inches from the wall.

3. Place the flashlight about 18 inches in front of the ball. Use the books to elevate the flashlight so that its light shines directly at the ball.

4. Use the drawing compass to inscribe a 2-inch circle on the poster paper.

5. Cut out the circle and tape it to one end of the second pencil.

6. Turn on the flashlight and darken the room.

7. Hold the pencil so that the paper circle is about 2 inches from the wall and to the right of the ball's shadow on the wall.

8. Slowly move the paper circle to the left so that it passes completely through the ball's shadow.

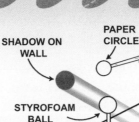

9. Notice the shape of the ball's shadow on the paper circle as the paper circle moves through the shadow.

10. Notice that at first only part of the paper circle (moon) is covered by the ball's (earth's) shadow. Next, the entire circle is covered. Last, the circle moves out of the shadow.

   What you have simulated is a **total lunar eclipse**. When the moon, earth, and sun are in a straight line, with the earth in the middle, the moon is completely hidden by the earth's shadow.

11. To simulate the movement of the moon with no eclipse, move the paper circle above or below the shadow the ball creates.

12. To simulate a **partial lunar eclipse**, move the circle so that about half of it moves through the ball's shadow. When only part of the moon passes into the earth's shadow, only a partial lunar eclipse is created.

But Columbus knew he was not welcome on Hispaniola. Sick at heart and in body, Columbus made plans to sail for Spain—as a passenger. On September 12, 1504, almost eight years from the day he first set eyes on the New World, Columbus was crossing back to the old one.

It was a stormy transit, one that took 56 days. On October 19, during a dreadful tempest, the mainmast of Columbus's vessel broke into four pieces. The gale threatened to capsize the ship. The Admiral could not rise from his bed on account of his gout. Yet, he was still able to issue instructions on how to jerry-rig a new mast from planks taken from the **stern** and **forecastle**.

On November 7, 1504, Columbus, along with his son Ferdinand, who was now 16 years old, arrived near Cadiz. The Admiral was home for good, having completed in two and a half years what he would always consider his *El Alto Viaje*, his High Voyage.

Ship damaged in a storm and sailors fighting to keep water off deck.
Thinkstock 125176213 (collection: Dorling Kindersley RF)

~ 8 ~

The Columbian Exchange

O N HIS RETURN TO Spain, Christopher Columbus was a sick, broken, and disabled man. With his exposure to the elements, chronic arthritis, gout, and bouts of malaria, the man from Genoa could barely stand, let alone walk. He was 52 years old—and it showed.

What the Admiral of the Ocean Sea now demanded was a royal accounting of what was owed to him. He also sought restoration of his rights. Columbus was not looking for approval from the monarchs—he knew the day for that had long passed.

Christopher Columbus had become a wealthy man. Gold was shipped back to him from Hispaniola, and he held vast tracts of land there. In today's dollars, the Admiral was probably worth more than $4 million. Still, Columbus felt he was due more, and he continued to press his demands whenever he could.

Christopher Columbus, Admiral of the Ocean Sea.

Thinkstock 1341738 (collection: iStockphoto)

When it came to money, Columbus's thoughts were not only of himself, however. In an act of kindness, he insisted that the men who accompanied him on his last voyage be paid what was owed them, even those who had rebelled on Jamaica. In a letter to his son Diego, who was attached to the royal court, the Admiral declared:

I turn to write a word for the attention of their Highnesses, begging them that they command pay be given to these men who were with me, for they are poor, and it goes on three years since they left their homes. The news which they bring back is more than great. They have passed through infinite perils and labors. . . . Speak of this to the Secretary of the Bishop, and to Juan Lopez and to whomsoever you find convenient. Your father who loves you more than himself.

When it came to restoration of his rights and titles, Columbus only partially succeeded. His case was not helped by the death of Queen Isabella on November 26, 1504, of an undetermined cancer. Of the two sovereigns, the queen was more supportive of Columbus. Without Isabella, the Admiral had to appeal to the king. Anything Columbus wanted from Ferdinand would be a tough sell.

In May 1505 Columbus, though now infirm, made his way to the royal court, traveling more than 500 miles on the back of a mule. King Ferdinand tried to convince Columbus to take a castle in Spain in exchange for his title claims. The Admiral refused.

King Ferdinand was not willing to grant Columbus all he wanted, even though Columbus's initial agreement with the Spanish Crown, the Capitulations, clearly assigned to the Admiral his titles. To concede to Columbus's demands would have made Columbus the richest man in the world. When the agreements were signed, back in 1492, the sovereigns had no way of knowing what the Admiral would discover or the vast financial implications of those discoveries.

A year later, in early May 1506, Christopher Columbus's health collapsed. On May 19, he took to his bed. A priest was called to administer last rites. Present at the Admiral's bedside were Diego and Ferdinand, his sons; Diego, Columbus's younger brother; and Diego Mendez and Bartolomeo Fieschi, loyal sailors and servants.

The next day, May 20, 1506, Columbus received the Holy Sacraments of the Catholic Church. As he lay dying, the lifelong sailor was heard to murmur, "Into thy hands Lord, I commend my spirit." He passed away at 54 years of age.

Though Christopher Columbus, the Admiral of the Ocean Sea, died a wealthy man, he passed away in obscurity. Centuries would pass before the full magnitude of his accomplishments was acknowledged.

Continued Exploration

WHEN COLUMBUS left Santo Domingo in 1504, there were already 10,000 Europeans living there. Much had changed in the dozen years since its founding. The whole island of Hispaniola had become a settled colony, an established Spanish outpost in what was clearly a New World.

But the early decades of the 16th century were still an age of discovery and exploration. As the Waldseemüller Map of 1507 (page 92) showed, to fill out the Western Hemisphere required intensive surveying. A number of explorers and conquistadors were eager to undertake the task.

Pedro Álvares Cabral, sailing for the Portuguese in 1500, left his homeland to follow Vasco da Gama's path to India. Whether by chance or on purpose, Cabral's fleet of 13 ships ventured out across the Atlantic in a wide arc. In so doing, Cabral made landfall on what he first assumed was a large island. Where Cabral touched was not an island, however, but the eastern bulge of South America. The explorer had discovered Brazil, which he was quick to claim for Portugal.

In 1513, Juan Ponce de León, who had been with Columbus on his second voyage, commanded an expedition in search of the so-called Fountain of Youth. Such a place supposedly existed somewhere in the Bahamas. De León never found the fountain, but in his hunt he landed on what is today Florida.

The routes of Ponce De León and Balboa.
Library of Congress, Geography and Map Division, Robertson's Geographic-Historical Series Illustrating the History of America and the United States: From 1492 to the Present g3701sm.gct077

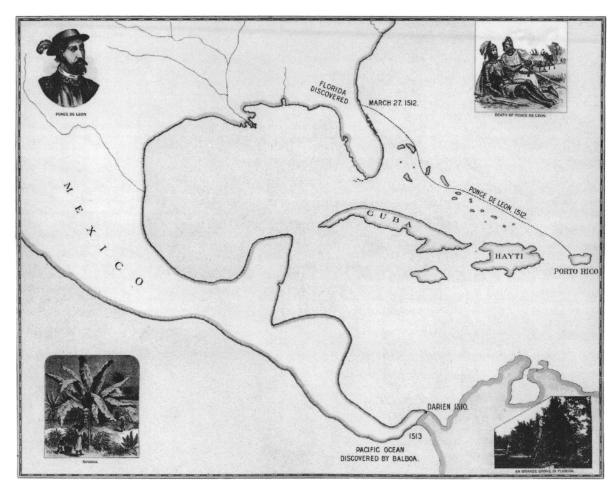

De León was the first European to explore a part of what became the United States.

Vasco Núñez de Balboa stowed away with his dog on a relief supply ship sailing for Panama in 1510. Befriending a local Indian chief and marrying his daughter, Balboa charmed the natives. In September 1513, the adventurer, with 190 Spanish soldiers, crossed the densest rain forest in the world. On September 25, he climbed a mountain peak and spied a vast sea. Balboa was thus the first European to look upon the eastern shore of the Pacific Ocean.

Hernando Cortés was only 18 when he sailed to Hispaniola. From there he joined a

(ABOVE) *Aztecs in canoes attacking a Spanish ship on Lake Texcoco.*
Thinkstock 112706719 (collection: Dorling Kindersley RF)

(RIGHT) *Spanish conquistadors looting Aztec treasure hidden inside a house.*
Thinkstock 112706767 (collection: Dorling Kindersley RF)

group of Spaniards who went on to subdue Cuba in 1511. Cortés, however, is best known for his conquest of the Aztecs in central Mexico, a bloody deed finally accomplished in 1521. Twenty years later, Cortés led an expedition against the Maya of Yucatan.

In September 1519, Ferdinand Magellan, a Portuguese sailing on behalf of Spain, left in an attempt to do what Columbus could only dream of—circumnavigate the world. Magellan began with five ships, which he took down the eastern coast of South America and around the horn into the Pacific. From there he sailed on across the vast ocean, eventually arriving on the island of Guam. The trip was hell on earth, as an officer noted in his logbook:

We have come through the straits and into the Pacific Ocean. We have spent three months and 20 days without any kind of fresh food. We were eating biscuits that were no longer biscuits but crumbs full of weevils and stinking of rats' urine. We were drinking yellowish water which had long been putrid. We also ate a few cow hides that covered the top of the main yard to prevent its chafing the rigging: but they had grown so hard, owing to the sun, the rain and the wind that we had to soak them in the sea for four to five days. We then put them on the embers for a time and that was how we managed to eat them. We also often ate sawdust. Rats were sold

for half a ducat each, but even at that price they were very hard to find.

Magellan himself never made the full trip around the world. He was killed by natives in the Philippines. Only one of the captain's five ships arrived back in Spain. Of the 250

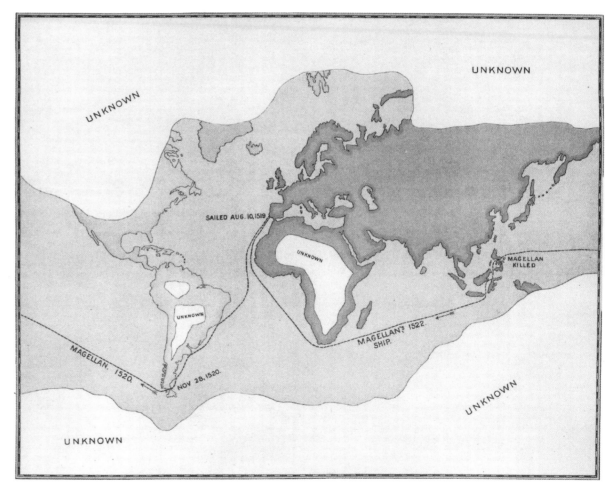

Magellan's voyages. Library of Congress, Geography and Map Division, Robertson's Geographic-Historical Series Illustrating the History of America and the United States: From 1492 to the Present g3701sm.gct077

✛ Was Christopher Columbus Jewish?

When Christopher Columbus sailed from Palos, Spain, on his first voyage on August 3, 1492, he put to sea a day late. Scheduled to depart on August 2, the Admiral held off because the harbor of Palos was jammed with dozens of ships trying to get out. They were filled with thousands of Jews, all of whom were being exiled from Spain, the result of a royal order to either become converts to Catholicism (*conversos*) or leave the country for good.

Some Jews who stayed and converted became known as **Marranos**, Jews who pretended to be Catholic in order to avoid religious persecution. On the outside they were Christians, yet in their homes, in hiding, they practiced Judaism. It has been alleged by some scholars that Christopher Columbus was a Marrano.

In support of their view, advocates point to the fact that in Columbus's will, he made provisions that one-tenth of his income be given to the poor and a dowry for poor girls be established—both acts are a part of Jewish customs. Columbus also decreed to give money to a Jew who lived near the entrance of the Jewish Quarter in Lisbon.

It is further alleged that, if correctly interpreted, Columbus's signature indicates the Admiral was a Jew.

Finally, it is pointed out that the real financiers of Columbus's first voyage, Louis de Santangel and Gabriel Sanchez, were supposedly Marranos.

In the end, Columbus, according to those who believe he was Jewish, undertook his explorations not for God, gold, and glory but to find a new homeland for Jews forced out of Spain. They would be settled, the thought was, in the New World.

There is no direct evidence to support assertions that Columbus was a Jew. The elements make for a good story, with an intriguing idea to back it up. But in reality, Columbus was probably as good a Catholic as there ever was. His most Catholic sovereigns, Ferdinand and Isabella, never suggested otherwise. Had they any doubt as to Columbus's true faith, there would have been no Spanish-sponsored voyages to seek a water route to Asia by sailing west.

men who had begun the epic journey, just 18 returned home. But, in so doing, they were the first ever to sail around the world.

There were other European discoverers in this age of exploration. Sailing north, south, east, and west, what they encountered, explored, and conquered changed the world. The most dramatic transition came with the interplay between two hemispheres—the Eastern and the Western. That mixing began on October 12, 1492, when Christopher Columbus first set foot in the New World.

The Great Exchange

IN 1972, Alfred W. Crosby, a professor at the University of Texas at Austin, published a small manuscript entitled *The Columbian Exchange* to little fanfare. Today, *The Columbian Exchange* is considered by many historians to describe one of the most spectacular and significant ecological events in the past thousand years.

The term Columbian Exchange refers to the interchange of plants, animals, cultures, human populations, transmittable diseases, and ideas between the Old World and the New. It began with Columbus, hence the name, and continues to this day.

Before Columbus, there were no bananas in Ecuador, no oranges in Florida, no coffee in Colombia, no cattle in Texas, no donkeys in Mexico, and no horses anywhere in North or South America. At the same time, there were no potatoes in Germany, no tomatoes in Italy, no chili peppers in India, no chocolate in Switzerland, and no cigarettes in France. The Columbian Exchange was the most massive swapping of plant life ever known.

The Exchange introduced to the Old World such calorie-rich foods as maize, cassava, white potatoes, and sweet potatoes. As a result, improvements in diet led to increased, denser populations, which in turn gave rise to larger cities.

Working the other way, the discovery of the New World provided the Old World with vast tracts of uncultivated land. New World soil, it turned out, was well suited to the cultivation of crops that Europeans had begun to raise back home. Foods such as coffee, soybeans, sugar, bananas, and oranges were introduced into the New World, where they flourished. Once harvested, the foods eventually reached markets all over the world.

In addition to crops, there arrived infectious diseases. From Europe came major killers, such as whooping cough, bubonic plague, chicken pox, measles, malaria, typhus, and smallpox. Native Americans had never encountered such diseases, and, as a consequence, had no immunity. The result was the near depopulation of the Western Hemisphere. It's estimated that 80 to 90 percent of the Native American populace was decimated within the 150 years following Columbus's first voyage.

The disease exchange favored Europe. That is, few New World diseases traveled to the Old—there simply weren't that many around to make the journey.

The one exception was venereal syphilis. Today, syphilis is a nonfatal affliction that can be treated effectively with penicillin. But in the late 15th and early 16th centuries, it was an outright killer. Christopher Columbus and his crew may have acquired syphilis from the Arawak of Hispaniola as a result of sexual contact. If so, they were the first to bring the disease east.

One crop that made it from the New World to the Old did not, at first, seem harmful, and was hardly seen as a disease. Native Americans probably began growing tobacco 2,000 years ago. For the most part, they smoked the plant during religious ceremonies. They may also have used it as a painkiller.

Europeans quickly adopted tobacco. At first it was actually thought of as medicine. Indeed, the French ambassador to Portugal, Jean Nicot de Villemain, from which the word "nicotine" comes, claimed it could cure almost any ailment. As time would tell, he couldn't have been more wrong.

MAKE AN OLD WORLD–NEW WORLD PIZZA

EXPLORERS FROM the Old World discovered not only a new land but also new foods that they had never seen before. They brought foods from the New World back to the Old World and exchanged foods from the Old World as well. This transfer of foods is known as the Columbian Exchange. Some of the foods we associate with certain Old World countries were actually found in the New World. Imagine . . . there was once no chocolate in Switzerland . . . no potatoes in Ireland, and . . . no tomatoes in Italy!

It actually took the Italians three centuries to accept the tomato as an edible fruit. They first started cooking it and making sauces in the 18th century. Imagine a world without pizza! Well, luckily you don't have to. Below is a recipe using Old World and New World ingredients to make a delicious Old World–New World Pizza.

This recipe uses premade, store-bought pizza dough. Take premade dough out of the refrigerator a few hours before you plan on using it to let it rise.

Adult supervision required

Materials

✛ Baking sheet
✛ Pastry brush
✛ Spatula
✛ Knife or pizza cutter
✛ 1 pound premade pizza dough
✛ 1 cup jarred pizza sauce
✛ 1 ¼ cups shredded mozzarella cheese

Old World Ingredients

✛ 1 tablespoon olive oil plus more for the baking sheet
✛ ¼ cup cooked broccoli
✛ ¼ cup cooked onion

New World Ingredients

✛ ¼ cup cooked and thinly sliced small potatoes
✛ ¼ cup sliced fresh tomato
✛ ¼ cup sliced zucchini
✛ ¼ cup of fresh or frozen (thawed) corn

1. Preheat oven to 450 degrees. Lightly oil a baking sheet. Stretch dough on prepared sheet and brush with oil, making sure to coat edges well. Spread a liberal amount of pizza sauce over the dough with a spatula. Top with shredded mozzarella cheese.

2. Top with remaining Old World and New World ingredients. Season with salt and pepper.

3. Bake pizza until browned, 20 to 25 minutes. Let cool for a few minutes before cutting pizza into desired slices and eating.

For better or worse, the food and disease interaction caused by the Columbian Exchange is an important legacy of the Columbus voyages. So, too, was the exchange of peoples. Europeans, for the most part, came to the New World voluntarily. Virtually all who arrived from Africa did not.

Dragged in Chains

FROM COLUMBUS'S very first voyage on, there was talk of enslaving Indians, either to work for the Spaniards coming to the New World or to be sent back to the Old World as servants. But the Arawak and other tribes of the Caribbean weren't accustomed to hard work in the tropical sun. They often escaped into the jungles and mountains. Many were prepared to commit suicide rather than accept enslavement. But with the discovery of gold on Hispaniola, demand for labor to work the mines was intense. Another source of supply, other than the locals, was required.

Governor Ovando may have been the first to bring enslaved Africans to the Caribbean in any quantity. In the beginning, it was an occasional slave here and there. But when it was discovered that Africans were good workers and that they were relatively immune to diseases, their numbers exploded. It was said that one black slave was equal to four Indians.

While gold was the initial lure in attracting African slave labor, it was the cultivation of Old World crops in the New World, such as coffee and sugar, that boosted slave demand. In the end, more than 12 million Africans may have been brought to the Americas between the 16th and 19th centuries. An untold additional number died in transit.

African slaves were not, at least in the beginning, as easily controlled as had been expected. As the writer Charles Mann wrote,

Faking sickness, working with deliberate lassitude [fatigue], losing supplies, sabotaging equipment, pilfering valuables, maiming the animals that hauled the cane, purposefully ruining the finished sugar— all were part of the furniture of plantation slavery.

When black slaves escaped into the mountains of Hispaniola, many could live out their lives in relative freedom. "Hidden by the forest from European eyes, they made it their business to wreck the industry that had enchained them," Mann continued. "For more than a century, African irregulars ranged unhindered over most of Hispaniola, funding their activities by covertly exchanging gold panned from

Slaves cultivating sugar cane in the West Indies.

mountain rivers with Spanish merchants for clothing, liquor, and iron."

Still, African slaves continued to arrive in the New World. The forced movement of such individuals reached its height in the 18th century. Then, in the 19th century it began to slow. In 1807, Britain passed the British Slave Trade Act, which banned the import of slaves into British colonies. With the passage, 30 years later, of the British Slavery Abolition Act, such bondage was abolished in every British colony. By the end of the 19th century, all forms of slavery were outlawed throughout the Western Hemisphere.

While the Colombian Exchange brought many advantages to both the Old and the New Worlds, the negative impacts cannot be ignored. Native Americans were depopulated by Old World diseases. With the loss of Indian labor, the hateful transatlantic African slave trade rose as an alternative source for workers. Most Americans are familiar with the adverse consequences of slavery in their own countries. What may not be appreciated

(LEFT) *Slaves coming aboard ship.* Thinkstock (photographer: Photo.com) 92844541 (collection: Photos.com)

(RIGHT) *Slaves ascending a mineshaft.* Thinkstock (photographer: Photo.com) 92837359 (collection: Photos.com)

is the impact such trade had on the African continent. The Colombian Exchange worked its way all around the world.

Changing the World

THE STORY'S validity is in doubt. The event depicted probably never happened. Still, it is a good story, and it tells us much about Christopher Columbus and his place in history.

When the Admiral of the Ocean Sea returned to Spain from his first voyage of discovery, he was hailed a hero. As the story goes, a banquet was held in Columbus's honor, given by a man named Pedro Gonzales de Mendoza, archbishop of Toledo and grand cardinal of Spain. In Girolamo Benzoni's *Historia del Mondo Nuovo*, the first Italian history of the New World, published in 1565, the tale is related as follows:

Columbus being at a party with many noble Spaniards, where, as was customary, the subject of the conversation was the Indies: one of them undertook to say: "Señor Cristóbal [Christopher Columbus], even if you had not undertaken this great enterprise, we should not have lacked a man who would have made the same discovery that you did, here in our own country of Spain, as it is full of great men clever in cosmography and

CREATE A GLOSSARY WORD SEARCH

ONE OF the best ways to familiarize yourself with the glossary words found in the back of this book is to create a glossary word search.

Materials

+ Graph paper
+ Ruler
+ Pencil with an eraser
+ Copy of the glossary (page 135)
+ Highlighter pen

1. Using your ruler, draw a square on your graph paper. The larger the square, the larger the puzzle, and the more words you will use.

2. Looking at the glossary, choose words that you will put inside the drawn square. As you write the word, use uppercase letters, one per square. You can write the word across, up and down, backward, or diagonally. Choose as many words as you like.

3. To the side of your square, keep a list of the words you are using so that players can know what to look for.

4. After you have written in all the words that you will want a player to find, fill in the blank squares with letters. Wherever possible, use short letter combinations that are part of some of the words you used. This will make the words easier to find.

5. Players should identify a word with a highlighter pen.

As a player identifies a word, he or she may want to read over the glossary definition.

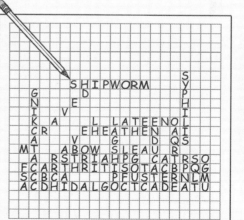

ADELANTADO
CARRACK
HIDALGO
GOUT
BOW
STERN
SYPHILIS
WESTERLIES
MALARIA
SHIPWORM
ISTHMUS
LATEEN
TACKING
DYSENTERY

literature." Columbus made no reply, but took an egg and had it placed on the table saying: "Gentlemen, you make it stand here, not with crumbs, salt, etc. (for anyone knows how to do it with meal or sand), but naked and without anything at all, as I will, who was the first to discover the Indies." They all tried, and no one succeeded in making it stand up. When the egg came round to the hands of Columbus, by beating it down on the table he fixed it, having thus crushed a little of one end; wherefore all remained confused, understanding what he meant: that after the deed is done, everybody knows how to do it; that they ought first to have sought for the Indies, and not laugh at him who had sought for them first.

✛ Columbus Myths

There are many myths surrounding Christopher Columbus. Four of them stand out. There is the myth that Columbus sailed west in 1492 to prove the world was round, and that he did so thanks to Queen Isabella's generosity in pawning her jewels to finance the enterprise. When Columbus arrived in the West Indies, it was said that it was he who discovered America, and that a thankless world left Columbus penniless, and he died a poor man.

Throughout, this book has sought to dispel these myths.

As has been shown, it wasn't a flat world that concerned Columbus's critics, but the size of the earth. His detractors, it turns out, were right and Columbus was wrong. The world was much greater in circumference than Columbus supposed. Had there not been a Western Hemisphere in the way, the Admiral would never have made it to far-off Asia.

Queen Isabella did offer to put her jewels up for collateral to finance the Enterprise of the Indies, but her offer was rejected. It was not necessary.

Norsemen, 500 years before Columbus, actually landed on the eastern coast of North America. The difference between them and Columbus, however, is that when the Admiral arrived, his countrymen stayed.

And, finally, rather than dying penniless, Columbus, by most standards, passed away a wealthy man. Indeed, the Admiral of the Ocean Sea argued long and, in time, successfully, to gain financial security for himself and his heirs. While Columbus did die in relative obscurity, he did not die a pauper.

There is no doubt that had Columbus not been the first European to sail to the West Indies, another navigator would have tried and succeeded. But this sort of thing is claimed for almost every major achievement, social as well as technical, that the world has witnessed. If Alexander Graham Bell had not invented the telephone, someone else would have. If Marie Curie's work had not led to chemotherapy, the most effective cancer treatment known, someone else's would have. If Frederick Douglass had not helped to change people's views about slavery forever, there were others who could have stepped forward.

Yet, it was Bell, Curie, and Douglass who actually did it. And in so doing, it was they who made history.

With all the controversy surrounding Christopher Columbus, with all the questioning and probing, there is one thing everybody can agree on: the Admiral of the Ocean Sea, Christopher Columbus, did indeed change the world.

Rewrite an Old Document

During Christopher Columbus's time, many documents were written in Latin. When translated into Old English, these texts can be difficult and confusing for modern English-language readers. Below is a paragraph written by the writer Peter Martyr in Latin. It was translated into English in 1555 by Richard Eden. The writing concerns the Indians of the West Indies and how some of them seemed to the Spaniards to be living in a so-called Golden Age of imagined simplicity and innocence. Try your hand at translating the document into more modern language.

Materials

✚ Pencil and paper

or

✚ Computer

Read the original document carefully. Then, either on paper or using a computer, translate, or rewrite, the document into something readable by you and your friends. Your rewritten document need not be a word-for-word translation. Just write a paragraph that will clarify the original, make it more understandable. An example clarification is given. Yours will undoubtedly look different—and possibly better. Good luck.

Original Paragraph as written by Richard Eden, in 1555:

And surely if they had receaued owre religion, I wolde thinke their life moste happye of all men, if they might therwith enioye their auncient libertie. A fewe thinges contente them, hauinge no delite in such superfluities, for the which in other places men take infinite paynes and commit manie vnlawfull actes, and yet are neuer satisfied, whereas many haue to muche, and none inowgh. But emonge these simple sowles, a fewe clothes serue the naked: weightes and measures are not needefull to such as can not skyll of crafte and deceyte and haue not the vse of pestiferous monye, the seede of innumerable myscheues. So that if we shall not be ashamed to confesse the truthe, they seeme to lyue in that goulden worlde of the whiche owlde wryters speake so much: wherin men lyued simplye and innocentlye without inforcement of lawes, without quarrellinge Iudges and libelles, contente onely to satisfie nature, without further vexation for knowledge of thinges to come.

AN EXAMPLE OF THE DOCUMENT REWRITTEN (YOURS NEED NOT BE THE SAME):

Though the Indians like being free, they would enjoy their lives even more if they became Catholics. They need only a few simple things to make them happy. The Indians do not care for luxuries. The men of Spain, however, love luxuries. Yet such craving for fine objects actually causes them great pain. This is particularly true if they have to commit crimes to get the money to pay for the luxuries. The men of Spain are never satisfied. Some have too much and some have too little. Yet among these simple Indians, only a few clothes make them happy. They do not need to count out everything since they are honest. No records of objects sold or bought are kept. The Indians seem to live in a golden world, the kind old Europeans often long for. This was a time when men lived simple, innocent lives, without the need to enforce laws. There was no fighting among each other. Such people just wanted to live simply. They did not want to worry or think about the future.

Websites to Explore

Christopher Columbus: Explorer

www.enchantedlearning.com/explorers/page/c
　/columbus.shtml

A good summary of the Admiral's four voyages. There are lots of maps to color, word puzzles to complete, and short writing assignments to do. Great for Columbus Day activities.

History.com: Christopher Columbus

www.history.com/topics/christopher-columbus

The site contains a number of short, excellent video clips on various aspects of the Christopher Columbus story, all from the History Channel. Examples include: Leif Eriksson vs. Christopher Columbus (time: 2:18); Columbus's Book of Privileges (time: 2:13); Columbus Uses the Skies to Survive (time: 3:25); Columbus's Mutinous Crew (time: 2:12), and Columbus's Quest for Gold (time 2:38).

Explorers—Navigation Tools

www.cccoe.net/lifeatsea/student/navtools.htm

Explorers at Sea allows you to investigate how ancient mariners navigated the ocean using various tools. See how the compass, maps, the astrolabe, the cross-staff, the quadrant, and the sextant were used during the Age of Exploration.

Life at Sea in the Age of Sail

www.rmg.co.uk/explore/sea-and-ships/facts
　/ships-and-seafarers/life-at-sea-in-the-age
　-of-sail

This site explores life on the ocean in the age of sail. Topics such as the following are vividly covered: "Why were punishments so harsh at sea?" "What were typical punishments?" "What food was there on board ships?" "What were the various jobs on board?" "What were press gangs?" "What sort of pay did seamen get?" Great reading!

History of Boats and Ships

www.historyworld.net/wrldhis/PlainText
   Histories.asp?historyid=aa14

The History of Boats and Ships covers boats and ships from Egypt and Mesopotamia (3,000 BC) to the early 19th century.

Columbus Day Activities, Lesson Plans, Songs, and Teaching Ideas

themes.atozteacherstuff.com/240/

This site is a great source of activities for Columbus Day. The site is aimed primarily at kindergarten through 5th grade, but there is material for all grades.

Arawak Indian Culture and History

www.native-languages.org/arawak_culture.htm

Arawak Indian Culture and History consists of numerous indexed links about the Arawak Indians and their society. The site emphasizes that while there is much Arawak history to examine, the Arawak Indians are alive today, a living people with a present and a future.

BBC—History—British History in Depth: Vasco da Gama

www.bbc.co.uk/history/british/tudors/vasco_da
   _gama_01.shtml

This site presents a full but readable account of the man who actually succeeded in what Christopher Columbus failed to do—find a direct water route from Europe to Asia.

Did Your Family Sail With Columbus?

www.flmnh.ufl.edu/caribarch/columbus.htm

This is an article that appeared in the July 7, 1991, issue of *Vista Magazine: The Magazine for All Hispanics*. It lists, as far as is known, the names of all those who sailed with Columbus on his first voyage. A separate list includes those that were left behind at La Navidad. While the author admits that the list is incomplete, it is interesting to read the names of those who actually sailed with the Admiral.

The Columbus Landfall Homepage

www.columbusnavigation.com/cclandfl.html

Here is a site that examines, after 500 years, the still-asked question: Where did Columbus actually land in the Western Hemisphere? It reviews some of the best-known theories and lets the reader be the judge.

Notes

Note to Readers

"As regards his exterior" Morison, *Admiral of the Ocean Sea*, 44–45

Chapter 1

"a Green Sea of Darkness" Thomas, *The Slave Trade*, 20

"There were men without heads" Lester, *The Fourth Part of the World*, 39

"So uncertain a thing" Colón cited in Keen, *The Life of Admiral Christopher Columbus*, 58

"He was the type of father" Morison, *Admiral of the Ocean Sea*, 12

"By San Fernando" Morison, *Admiral of the Ocean Sea*, 44

"growing up he was" Fernández-Armesto, *Columbus*, 25

"I made sail at night" Fernández-Armesto, *Columbus*, 27

He is said to have sat glum faced. Bergreen, *Columbus*, 71

"much beyond the limit" Fernández-Armesto, *Columbus*, 25

"A lady named doña Felipa Moniz" Colón cited in Keen, *Christopher Columbus*, 14

Chapter 2

"So that from thenceforth" Fernández-Armesto, *1492*, 184

"They have the greatest abundance" Landström, *Columbus*, 31

"The King, as he observed" Morison, *Admiral of the Ocean Sea*, 71

"Empowered henceforward to call" Morison, *Admiral of the Ocean Sea*, 105

"Lacking the knowledge" Di Giovanni, *Christopher Columbus*, 87

"Take Beatriz Enríquez in your charge" Di Giovanni, *Christopher Columbus*, 92

"I will not glorify Spain" Morison, *Admiral of the Ocean Sea*, 101

"He told her he was" Di Giovanni, *Christopher Columbus*, 101

Chapter 3

"well suited for the enterprise" Morison, *Admiral of the Ocean Sea*, 131

"because more could be gained" Di Giovanni, *Christopher Columbus*, 123

"They aught to make good" Di Giovanni, *Christopher Columbus*, 123

"These people" Morison, *Admiral of the Ocean Sea*, 233

"The island is filled with" Di Giovanni, *Christopher Columbus*, 133

"none too good" Morison, *Admiral of the Ocean Sea*, 255

"These people have no spears" Di Giovanni, *Christopher Columbus*, 151

"Our Lord had caused" Landström, *Columbus*, 94

Chapter 4

"In the Year 734" Lester, *The Fourth Part of the World*, 210

"a great ambulatory (moveable) meat locker" Mann, *1491*, 181

"Then you just follow" Mann, *1491*, 181

"The Inca maintained a road" Fernández-Armesto, *1492*, 304

"They are so ingenuous" Morison, *Admiral of the Ocean Sea*, 231

"Following hard on the heels" Johnson, *The Story of the Caribs and Arawaks, Part I*, 1

"We inquired of the women" Fernández-Armesto, *Columbus*, 118

"a people called Cannibales" Johnson, *The Story of the Caribs and the Arawaks, Part 4*, 2

"they [the Caribs] may be captured" *The Story of the Caribs and the Arawaks*, Part 4, 2

"That Venetian of ours" Lester, *The Fourth Part of the World*, 284

Chapter 5

"There were wild fruit" Di Giovanni, *Christopher Columbus*, 203

"From that point on" Di Giovanni, *Christopher Columbus*, 241

"When we reached the waters" Di Giovanni, *Christopher Columbus*, 250

"Of the valley that was" Sale, *The Conquest of Paradise*, 154

"Even the cruelest of the Turks" Bergreen, *Columbus*, 203

"Oppressed by the impossible requirement" Bergreen, *Columbus*, 204

"They had given up" Bergreen, *Columbus*, 204

"It is hardly surprising" Sale, *The Conquest of Paradise*, 156

"Where could they have been put" Sale, *The Conquest of Paradise*, 167

Chapter 6

"It never was our intention" Di Giovanni, *Christopher Columbus*, 268

"The Admiral was suddenly" Di Giovanni, *Christopher Columbus*, 274

"So suddenly and unexpectedly" Di Giovanni, *Christopher Columbus*, 276

"His Divine Majesty ever showeth" Di Giovanni, *Christopher Columbus*, 277

"There came a current from" Di Giovanni, *Christopher Columbus*, 279

"I have before me a mighty" Di Giovanni, *Christopher Columbus*, 286

"Don Cristóbal Colón [Christopher Columbus]" Landström, *Columbus*, 152

"In Spain, they judge me" Landström, *Columbus*, 153

"He had been placed in chains" Di Giovanni, *Christopher Columbus*, 302

"Sign with my signature" Morison, *Admiral of the Ocean Sea*, 356

Chapter 7

"The storm was terrible" Dugard, *The Last Voyage of Columbus*, 128

"My people were very weak" Di Giovanni, *Christopher Columbus*, 323

"Crying in a trembling voice" Dugard, *The Last Voyage of Columbus*, 202

"We stood over toward Jamaica" Di Giovanni, *Christopher Columbus*, 351

"Having got in" Di Giovanni, *Christopher Columbus*, 357

"The Porras brothers and their merry" Morison, *Admiral of the Ocean Sea*, 653

Chapter 8

"I turn to write a word" Di Giovanni, *Christopher Columbus*, 376

"Into thy hands Lord" Bergreen, *Columbus*, 362

"We have come through the straits" Boorstin, *The Discoverers*, 265

"Faking sickness" Mann, *1493*, 302

"Hidden by the forest" Mann, *1493*, 302

"Columbus being at a party" Morison, *Admiral of the Ocean Sea*, 36

"And surely if they had" Morison, *Admiral of the Ocean Sea*, 232

Glossary

adelantado Governor of a recently conquered province

Admiral of the Ocean Sea One who exercises admiralty jurisdiction, that is, control over a naval crew, while at sea

alcalde mayor A mayor of a Spanish or Spanish-American town who acts as an extension of royal governance

archipelago A group or chain of many islands

arthritis Painful inflammation of the joints, particularly in the hands and feet

bow The front end of a ship

cacique A Spanish American or Indian chief

canalla Low-class, despicable person, usually of criminal background

caravel A small 15th- and 16th-century sailing ship, usually with three masts with triangular or square sails

carrack A medium-size 15th- and 16th-century merchant sailing ship

cartographer A person whose work is making maps or charts

cassava A tropical American plant with edible, starchy roots

crow's nest A partly enclosed platform high on a ship's mast used as a lookout

dead reckoning The determination of distance and course from the record of course sailed, without the aid of celestial observation

doldrums A part of the ocean near the equator abounding in calms

doublet A close-fitting jacket

ducat A Spanish gold coin during Columbus's time, worth approximately $37 in 2010 dollars

dynastic An adjective used to describe a period during which a certain family reigns

dysentery A disease causing severe diarrhea, usually caused by an infection

encomienda A grant of an allotment of Indians who were to serve the holder with tribute and labor

fathom A unit of measure used for the depth of water equal to 6 feet

fief Land held from a lord that is worked by peasants in return for service

flagship The ship in a squadron that carries the commander

flotilla A fleet of boats or ships

forecastle The front part of a merchant ship, where the crew's quarters are located

galleass A large, three-masted vessel having sails and oars and carrying heavy guns

gnomon An object that by its position or the length of its shadow serves as an indicator (as with use in a sundial)

gout Painful swelling of the joints with uric acid

grommet A slang term referring to a ship's cabin boy

gulfweed A seaweed of tropical American seas

habit A distinctive religious costume, usually of rough cloth, worn for certain occasions

harquebus An early type of portable gun

hawk's bell A small brass bell, which falconers in Europe tied to the legs of their hunting birds, and which proved to be a popular object of barter by the Spaniards

heathen An unconverted person who does not acknowledge the God of the New Testament

hidalgo A member of the lower nobility of Spain

horticulturalist One who grows vegetables in a garden or an orchard

hull The frame or body of a ship, excluding the masts, rigging, superstructure, etc.

isthmus A narrow strip of land connecting two larger land areas

keel The entire length of the bottom of a boat or ship and supporting the frame

knot A unit of speed of one nautical mile (6,076 feet) an hour

lateen A triangular sail extended by a long spar slung to a low mast

league A distance measurement equivalent to about 3.45 miles

lunar eclipse A situation in which the moon is hidden by the shadow of the earth as it blocks light from the sun

malaria A human disease transmitted by the bite of the anopheline mosquito, causing periodic attacks of chills and fever

maravedi A Spanish copper coin during Columbus's time, worth approximately 11 cents in 2010 dollars

mariner A sailor or seaman

Marrano A Jew pretending to be a Christian

martyr A person who chooses to suffer or die rather than give up his or her faith

nautical mile A unit of measurement (equal to 6,076 feet) that is based on the circumference of the Earth at the equator

Pillars of Hercules The strait between North Africa and southern Spain that also separates the Atlantic Ocean and the Mediterranean Sea

pilot A person licensed to direct ships into or out of a harbor or through difficult waters

placer River deposits containing valuable minerals, such as gold

poop deck A partial deck above a ship's main rear deck

Renaissance The humanistic revival of classical influence expressed in the flowering of the arts, literature, and the beginnings of modern science from the 14th to the 17th century in Europe

repartimiento An assignment of Indians or land to a Spanish settler during the first years of colonization in the New World

run aground When a ship gets stuck on shore, as its hull scrapes the sea bottom

sargassum A floating brown algae found in tropical seas

sepulcher A small, sealed cavity, holding a martyrs' relics

shipworm A marine clam that burrows into submerged wood and causes great damage to wooden ships

statute mile A unit of measure equal to 5,280 feet

stern The rear end of a ship

stipend A regular or fixed payment for services

strait A comparatively narrow passageway connecting two large bodies of water

syphilis A chronic, contagious, sexually transmitted disease, treatable today, but often fatal in Columbus's day

tacking Changing direction by turning a ship's bow into the wind

terra firma Dry land or solid ground

trade To engage in the exchange, purchase, or sale of goods

tribute A regular payment made by one ruler to another as acknowledgment of submission

viceroy The governor of a country or province who rules as the representative of a king or sovereign

vortex Something that resembles a whirlpool

watch A portion of time during which a part of a ship's company is on duty

westerlies Winds coming from the west

yautia An edible, starchy tropical plant

Bibliography

Bergreen, Laurence. *Columbus: The Four Voyages.* New York: Viking, 2011.

Bernstein, William J. *A Splendid Exchange: How Trade Shaped the World from Prehistory to Today.* New York: Atlantic Monthly Press, 2008.

Boorstin, Daniel J. *The Discoverers.* New York: Random House, 1983.

Cei, Lia Pierotti. *Christopher Columbus: The Italian Who Changed the History of the World.* Milano: Fabbri Editori, Regione Liguria, 1985.

Cohen, J. M., ed. *The Four Voyages of Christopher Columbus.* New York: Penguin Books, 1969.

Colón Ferdinand. *The Life of Admiral Christopher Columbus.* Translated and annotated by Benjamin Keen. New Brunswick: Rutgers University Press, 1992.

Delouche, Frédéric, ed. *Illustrated History of Europe: A Unique Portrait of Europe's Common History.* New York: H. Holt, 1993.

Diamond, Jared. *Collapse: How Societies Choose to Fail or Succeed.* New York: Viking, 2005.

———. *Guns, Germs, and Steel: The Fates of Human Societies.* New York: W. W. Norton & Company, 1998.

Di Giovanni, Mario. *Christopher Columbus: His Life and Discoveries.* San Gabriel, CA: Columbus Explorers, Inc., 1991.

Dugard, Martin. *The Last Voyage of Columbus.* New York: Little, Brown and Co., 2005.

Eakin, Marshall C. *The History of Latin America: Collision of Cultures.* New York: Palgrave Macmillan, 2007.

Fernández-Armesto, Felipe. *1492: The Year the World Began*. New York: HarperCollins, 2009.

Irving, Washington. *The Discovery and Conquest of the New World (Containing the Life and Voyages of Christopher Columbus)*. Nashville: Central Publishing House, 1892.

Jones, Mary Ellen. *Christopher Columbus and His Legacy: Opposing Viewpoints*. San Diego: Greenhaven Press, Inc., 1992.

Las Casas, Bartolomé de. *Tears of the Indians*. New York: Oriole Editions, 1970.

Lester, Toby. *The Fourth Part of the World*. New York: Free Press, 2009.

Mann, Charles C. *1491: New Revelations of the Americas before Columbus*. New York: Knopf, 2005.

———. *1493: Uncovering the New World Columbus Created*. New York: Alfred. A. Knopf, 2011.

Morison, Samuel Eliot. *Admiral of the Ocean Sea: A Life of Christopher Columbus*. Boston: Little, Brown and Co., 1942.

Murphy, Dallas. *Rounding the Horn*. New York: Basic Books, 2004.

Page, Jake. *In the Hands of the Great Spirit: The 20,000-Year History of American Indians*. New York: Free Press, 2003.

Prescott, William H. *History of the Conquest of Mexico & History of the Conquest of Peru*. New York: The Modern Library, 1843.

Sale, Kirkpatrick. *The Conquest of Paradise: Christopher Columbus and the Colombian Legacy*. New York: Knopf, 1990.

Thomas, Hugh. *The Slave Trade: The Story of the Atlantic Slave Trade, 1440–1870*. New York: Simon & Schuster, 1997.

Utley, Robert M. and Wilcomb E. Washburn. *Indian Wars*. New York: American Heritage, 1977.

Winchester, Simon. *Atlantic*. New York: HarperCollins, 2010.